First World War
and Army of Occupation
War Diary
France, Belgium and Germany

36 DIVISION
Divisional Troops
Divisional Trench Mortar Batteries
1 August 1916 - 28 February 1919

WO95/2496/7

The Naval & Military Press Ltd
www.nmarchive.com
Published in association with The National Archives

Published by

The Naval & Military Press Ltd

Unit 10 Ridgewood Industrial Park,

Uckfield, East Sussex,

TN22 5QE England

Tel: +44 (0) 1825 749494

www.naval-military-press.com

www.nmarchive.com

This diary has been reprinted in facsimile from the original. Any imperfections are inevitably reproduced and the quality may fall short of modern type and cartographic standards.

© Crown Copyright
Images reproduced by permission of The National Archives, London, England, 2015.

Contents

Document type	Place/Title	Date From	Date To
Heading	WO95/2496		
Heading	36th Division. Divl Trench Mortar Batts. Aug 1916-Feb 1919		
War Diary	S.23.a.7.6	01/08/1916	31/08/1916
War Diary	In The Field.	03/09/1916	30/09/1916
War Diary	In The Field.	01/09/1916	27/09/1916
War Diary	In The Field.	09/09/1916	24/09/1916
War Diary	In The Field.	10/09/1916	30/09/1916
War Diary	In The Field.	26/09/1916	30/09/1916
Heading	War Diary of V 36 Trench Mortar Battery 36 Division For October 1916		
War Diary	In The Field.	02/10/1916	31/10/1916
Heading	War Diary of X 36 Trench Mortar Battery For October 1916		
War Diary	R.E. Farm.	01/10/1916	31/10/1916
War Diary	In The Field.	02/10/1916	31/10/1916
War Diary	In The Field.	01/10/1916	31/10/1916
War Diary	R.E. Farm.	01/11/1916	30/11/1916
War Diary	In The Field.	02/12/1916	15/12/1916
War Diary	In The Field.	08/12/1916	28/04/1917
War Diary	In The Field.	20/04/1917	06/06/1917
War Diary	Field.	06/06/1917	12/08/1917
War Diary	Field.	11/08/1917	07/12/1917
War Diary	Field.	05/12/1917	15/01/1918
War Diary	Field.	14/01/1918	31/01/1918
War Diary	Field.	20/01/1918	28/02/1918
Heading	36th Divisional Artillery. Trench Mortar Officer 36th Division. March 1918		
Miscellaneous	36th Div. G.X. 20/462. D.A.G. 3rd Echelon.	29/07/1918	29/07/1918
War Diary		01/03/1918	31/03/1918
Miscellaneous	Trench Mortars.		
Heading	36th Divisional Artillery. X & Y Trench Mortar Batteries 36th Division. April 1918		
War Diary	La Rue St Pierre Auchy La Montagne Charny.	01/04/1918	07/04/1918
War Diary	Courselles.	08/04/1918	10/04/1918
War Diary	Pont De Metz.	11/04/1918	14/04/1918
War Diary	Godewaersvelde	15/04/1918	23/04/1918
War Diary	Hamhoek.	24/04/1918	24/04/1918
War Diary	Peselhoek.	25/04/1918	10/05/1918
War Diary	C.25.c.9.9	12/05/1918	18/05/1918
War Diary	Sheet 28 N.W. 20,000	19/05/1918	31/05/1918
Heading	36th Divisional T.M. Batteries. War Diary June 1918. Ref. Sheet 28 N.W. 27 N.E.		
Miscellaneous			
War Diary	Ref Sheet 28 N.W.	01/06/1918	06/06/1918
War Diary	Ref Sheet.	07/06/1918	16/06/1918
War Diary	Ref Sheet 28 N.W.	17/06/1918	27/06/1918
War Diary	Sheet 27 N.E.	28/06/1918	30/06/1918
Heading	36th Divisional. T.M. Batteries War Diary July 1918. Ref. Sheet 28. 27		

Miscellaneous War Diary		Ref Sheet 28. 27	01/07/1918	31/07/1918
Heading		36th Divisional. T.M. Batteries. War Diary August 1918		
Miscellaneous War Diary			01/08/1918	31/08/1918
Heading		36th Divisional. T.M. Batteries. War Diary September 1918		
Miscellaneous War Diary			01/09/1918	30/09/1918
Heading		36th Divisional Trench Mortar Batteries War Diary October 1918. Ref Sheet 28. 29. Vol.28		
War Diary		Ref Sheet 28	01/10/1918	31/10/1918
Heading		36th Divisional Trench Mortar. War Diary November 1918. Ref Sheet 29. Vol.29		
Miscellaneous War Diary			01/11/1918	30/11/1918
Heading		36th Divisional Trench Mortar. War Diary December 1918		
Miscellaneous War Diary		Tourcoing	01/12/1918	13/12/1918
War Diary		Courtrai.	13/12/1918	31/12/1918
War Diary		Mouscron.	01/02/1919	16/02/1919
War Diary		Mouscron.	01/02/1919	28/02/1919
War Diary			17/02/1919	28/02/1919

w095/2496

36TH DIVISION

DIVL TRENCH MORTAR BATTS.
AUG 1916-FEB 1919

36TH DIVISION

Vol 1

Army Form C. 2118

36th Divisional Trench Mortar Batteries
Lt. Colonel H.C. Johnston RFA Comdg.

WAR DIARY or INTELLIGENCE SUMMARY
(Erase heading not required.)

Instructions regarding War Diaries and Intelligence Summaries are contained in F.S. Regs., Part II. and the Staff Manual respectively. Title Pages will be prepared in manuscript.

Place	Date	Hour	Summary of Events and Information	Remarks and references to Appendices
S.23 & 7.6	August 7/6	12-6pm	X/36, Y/36, Z/36 TM Batteries & V/36 H.T.M. Bty in action supporting gun positions	
		7pm	Y/36 go into action with 3 guns at N.36.c 60.70, N.36.c 60.60, & V.1.c 40.90, the remaining position at T.6 & 25.70 being in course of construction	
	7/8		Y/36 engaged on afternoon of 7th in ranging of 8th firing 43 rds. Enemy retaliation heavily with T.M.s & Rifle Grenades. En. Cooperation with our Stokes batteries. Enemy's fire was silenced.	
	8th		V/36 H.T.M. moved kittens to COURT E JREVE T'ARM	
	9	9:15	Y/36 in action under heavy trench warfare conditions. During this period 184 rds were fired in retaliation.	
			No 2.1366 Dr PROSSER G.F. Y/36 slightly wounded in action	
			No 27405 Lt PAINTER A.E. Y/36 " " "	
	12th		Z/36 go into action with 1 gun at U.14.d 65.65	
	14th		U.14.d 65.60 & U.8.d 25.30 being in course of construction	
	16		Y/36 fired 54 rds on enemy's Front line & support trenches in cooperation with a pre-arranged bombardment by the 19th Division	
	17th		No 27735 Bdr CARVER F. Y/36 severely wounded in action	
	19		Y/36 fired 27 rds in retaliation to hostile T.M's eventually silenced by our artillery.	
	20		Y/36 fired 85 rds " " against hostile T.M's which appeared to be firing from	
	20-28		FACTORY T'ARM and JACKSONS T'ARM. hostile H.T.M's machine guns repulsed by infantry as pried out to action	
	25		Z/36 slightly firing 111 rds	
	27		X/36 " " " 2 19th Division	
	28		Y/36 fired 30 rds in retaliation to hostile T.M. fire	
	30		Y/36 fired 111 rds., Z/36 fired 30 rds in retaliation for hostile T.M. fire	
	31		Z/36 fired 16 rds. Y/36 fired 43 rds during the day in cooperation with a rearranged plan of R.N. Engineers	
	31		No 30462 Gnr STOCKWELL A.E. Y/36 H.T.M. Bty killed by shell fire at COURTE JREVE FARM	

H.C. Johnston, LT. COL. COMDG.
154 BRIGADE R.F.A.

WAR DIARY

INTELLIGENCE SUMMARY

Army Form C. 2118

Y 36 Trench Mortar Battery

Place	Date Sept	Hour	Summary of Events and Information	Remarks and references to Appendices
In the field	3		Three men of D.A.C. who has been receiving instruction in the line returned to their unit.	
	5		Fired 56 rounds between 5.30 & 6.50 p.m. Cutting wire from N 36 D 20.75 to N 36 D 30.40. Three good gaps were made. Enemy threw over 6 or 9 "oil cans" from direction of N 36 D 95.15, practically no retaliation on our fire.	
	6		From 3 p.m. to 3.50 p.m. an artillery barely bombards factory farm. With two guns we fired 18 rounds on factory farm, front line trenches wire north of the farm. Receives no retaliation.	
	7		Fired with success 36 rounds on dug outs at factory farm & 22 rounds on front line & wire at N 36 D 20.75. No retaliation.	
	9		At 4.20 p.m. fires 4 rounds for registration purposes. The Boche replies with 9 Minenwerfers, but we silenced him by firing another 29. No firing of any kinds during the day. Replying to our Stokes at 12 midnight enemy sent over several 5.9's & three Minenwerfers. Flash of enemy mortar seen behind the Bastion at about N 36 D 5.8.	Aug '16 Feb '19
	10		Fires 6 rounds for registration on N 36 D 25.75. The Boche retaliates with a couple of Minenwerfers. We immediately opens & eventually silences enemy sending over about two to one.	
	11			
	14		Rain impedes work on new positions, it being impossible to drain water out of ammunition recesses.	

WAR DIARY
or
INTELLIGENCE SUMMARY

(Erase heading not required.)

Army Form C. 2118

Y 36 Trench Mortar Battery

Place	Date Sept	Hour	Summary of Events and Information	Remarks and references to Appendices
In the fields	15		Rain again considerably interferes with work on new positions. Enemy sent over several Minenwerfers to which we retaliated – time 5.30 p.m. At night 2 we retaliates to enemy, firing on his front & support lines has positions were completed.	II
	16			
	17		Opened fire with 3 guns at 11 a.m. on N 36 A & N all fires 110 rounds, the Boche replying with a few Minenwerfers.	
	18		Twice during the day – at 12.15 a.m. & 11 p.m. – we silences enemy Mortar fire.	
	20		Rain caused considerable portion of new position to fall in. Enemy put over a few mortars at 11.30 a.m.; our retaliation caused him to cease fire. The same thing happens at 2.30 in the afternoon. 2/Lt Dickson DY 117 Bde reports for temporary duty with the Bty.	
	22		Between 4.30 p.m. & 4.50 p.m., in conjunction with the Stokes mortars, we sent over 16 rounds to Factory Farm.	
	23		Using three guns we sent over 103 bombs to N 36 D 7.3. Enemy retaliates with mortars, artillery of all calibre & a number of rifle grenades.	
	24		At 6.30 a.m. the Hun, replying to our Stokes, sent over 9 mortars & several rifle grenades. We silences him with 25 bombs.	
	25.		Between 6.30 & 7.30 p.m. the enemy put over 6 T.M.'s & some grenades & we retaliates with 23 rounds on the Bastion & Factory Farm.	

Army Form C. 2118

WAR DIARY
INTELLIGENCE SUMMARY
(Erase heading not required.)

Y 36 Trench Mortar Battery

Instructions regarding War Diaries and Intelligence Summaries are contained in F.S. Regs., Part II. and the Staff Manual respectively. Title Pages will be prepared in manuscript.

Place	Date Sept	Hour	Summary of Events and Information	Remarks and references to Appendices
In the fields	26		During the morning we silenced the Boche who sent over a few Minenwerfers and in afternoon registered with 5 rounds on N 36 D 71.06.	III
	28		Took part in Group operation between 9 a.m. & 10.25 a.m. firing on N 36 D 71.06 & on wire & trenches from N 36 D 20.77 to N 36 D 15.90 — in all 54 rounds. The Boche sent over several Minenwerfers just before our bombardment commenced, working on fire appeared as took life immediate & intense retaliation.	
	29		Fired 17 rounds in registering on wire at N 36 D 71.06; practically no retaliation. Several men from D.A.C. returned to their unit upon completion of course.	
	30		From 12 noon to 1.15 p.m. fired 49 rounds at wire N 36 D 71.06. Enemy retaliating with 5.9's.	

J A Price 2/Lieut R.F.A
O/C., Y 36 T.M. Battery.

Army Form C. 2118

WAR DIARY
INTELLIGENCE SUMMARY J 36 Trench Mortar Battery
(Erase heading not required.)

Instructions regarding War Diaries and Intelligence Summaries are contained in F. S. Regs., Part II. and the Staff Manual respectively. Title Pages will be prepared in manuscript.

Place	Date Sept-	Hour	Summary of Events and Information	Remarks and references to Appendices
In the Field	1		One gun in action at Antoni's Farm. Work proceeding on new position. New position completed & second gun got into action.	
	14			
	15		Both guns handed over to 19th Division.	
	17		Battery moved from bivouacs at Hyde Park Corner to T.M.H.Q. T.16.A.2.8. Gabion Farm position repaired & two guns taken into action by night.	
	18			
	19		60 rounds fired in Group operations on la Petite Douve Farm. Building material taken by night party to Boyle's Farm.	
	22		Two temporary positions at Boyle's Farm completed.	
	25		Two guns got into action at Boyle's Farm.	
	26		Fired 120 rounds in Group operations. Firing commenced at 9 a.m. & concluded at 10.25 a.m. — Intervals of 15 minutes. Enemy fire — nil.	
	27		Guns taken out of action at night.	

[signature] 2/Lt. R.F.A.
O/C., J 36 T. M. Battery.

French Morteau
Vol 2

WAR DIARY
INTELLIGENCE SUMMARY
(Erase heading not required.)

Army Form C. 2118

X 36. Trench Mortar Battery

Instructions regarding War Diaries and Intelligence Summaries are contained in F.S. Regs., Part II. and the Staff Manual respectively. Title Pages will be prepared in manuscript.

Place	Date Sept	Hour	Summary of Events and Information	Remarks and references to Appendices
In the field	9		Came out of action in the salient having over on four guns to "Z" 3rd Canadian T.M. Bty.	
	11		The Battery arrives from the salient & took over two guns from 19th Division near R.E. Farm; also 193 rounds of ammunition.	
	13		Arrives at new camp T.16.a.2.8.	
	16		Opened fire at 10.30 a.m., expending 104 rounds by 12 noon. Fires again at 2.30 (46 rounds). At midnight enemy opens bombardment lasting about one hour — mostly on our left.	
	17		There was a little enemy trench mortaring in forenoon; this was quickly silenced by our artillery. Covers by artillery, fires 19 rounds in the afternoon. Enemy shells small wood h.35.B.75.30 with 77 mm. shrapnel from 8.30 a.m. to 11 a.m. He also sent over 4 Minenwerfer. We retaliates with 14 rounds doing much damage on N.36.a.50.40 & 50.60.	
	20			
	22		Bombards enemy lines N.36.A with 2 guns firing 115 bombs in one hour — 3 p.m. to 4 p.m. Enemy shelles buildings in N.36.A doing considerable damage. Enemy retaliates with 4 Minenwerfer here on our position.	
	24		Enemy trench mortars active from 6 a.m. to 7 a.m., but heavies & Trench M. Bty fires 22 rounds on enemy support line N.36.A. At 10 a.m. a hostile aeroplane, which appears over our lines, was driven back.	

WAR DIARY

Army Form C. 2118

INTELLIGENCE SUMMARY V 36 Heavy Trench Mortar Battery

(Erase heading not required.)

Place	Date Sept.	Hour	Summary of Events and Information	Remarks and references to Appendices
In the field	10		Handed over positions under construction near Anton's Farm to 19th Division. Took over gun in action & 23 rounds of ammunition near R.E. Farm from 19th Division.	
	16		Took part in Left Group operations. Fired 40 rounds on enemy support line during the 4 hours. Enemy retaliation very weak. Gun fires about 140 yds under map range, but fires uniformly; two rounds were blind. 2/Lieut R.L. Hadden posted to the Battery in place of 2/Lieut T. McComb who was evacuated.	
	19			
	22		Fires 13 rounds on enemy support line – Left Group operations. Gun fires about 160 yards below map range. Enemy retaliates mainly with heavy & light Minenwerfers & 10 cm. This retaliation was not heavy.	
	26		Left Group operations – fires 13 rounds on enemy support line. Enemy retaliates with heavy & light Minenwerfer, 77 m.m. & 10 c.m.; heavy for 20 minutes, but then practically ceases.	
	30		Positions near Durham Road & Gooseberry Farm nearing completion with the exception of the ammunition recesses. We have been very much hindered by the inflow of water.	

R. Powell
Capt. R.F.A.,
O/C., V 36 H.T.M. Bty.

Army Form C. 2118

WAR DIARY
~~INTELLIGENCE SUMMARY~~ X 36 Trench Mortar Battery
(Erase heading not required.)

Instructions regarding War Diaries and Intelligence Summaries are contained in F.S. Regs., Part II. and the Staff Manual respectively. Title Pages will be prepared in manuscript.

Place	Date Sept	Hour	Summary of Events and Information	Remarks and references to Appendices
Trenches	26		Enemy sent over 6 Minenwerfers; we retaliated with 20 rounds — effect good.	II
	28		Bombardes enemy front & second lines N 36 A 52-50 to N 36 A 50.60. Fired 150 rounds with 3 guns in 45 minutes. Firing was very accurate & damage done was great. Feeble retaliation by enemy with Minenwerfers & 77 h.v. shells.	
	30		The enemy sent over two large Minenwerfers close to one gun; time 3.15 p.m. One Stokes mortar was burried. We retaliated with 114 rounds on enemy support line N 36 A behind point 59.	

J. Melchkindale 2/Lieut R.F.A.
O/C. X 36 T.M. Battery

War Diary
of
V 36 Trench Mortar Battery
36 Division
for
October 1916.

V36 Heavy T.M. By.

WAR DIARY for Month of October

INTELLIGENCE SUMMARY

Army Form C. 2118

Place	Date	Hour	Summary of Events and Information	Remarks and references to Appendices
In the field	2 Oct. 1916.		Preparation and strengthening of R.E. Farm position commenced.	
	4.	8.30 a.m.	Fired 12 rounds from R.E. Farm position (left group operators). Enemy retaliation heavy at first, but no extensive damage. Gun fires somewhat erratically, and one round was short.	
	12.	4 a.m.	Gun taken up and mounted in Gooseberry Farm position.	
	17.	4 p.m.	Fired 30 rounds from R.E. Farm position and 18 rounds from Gooseberry Farm position. One round from R.E. Farm dropped and exploded 25 yds from Gun-pit but did no damage. One round from Gooseberry Farm was short. Enemy retaliation heavy.	
	19.		50 men detailed for works with Medium T.M. Btys.	
	20.		Gooseberry Farm position flooded. 6½ feet of water in ammunition store.	
	21.		Plumbing day and night. Started work at O.P. on Hill 49.	
	22.		Detailed from V36 and attached to X, Y, & Z 36 Btys. Gun pit and ammunition stores at Gooseberry Farm pumped dry, and trench leading to position flooded with a 12 feet dam.	
	24.		15 yards of trench leading to Durham Road position fell in, closing	

V/36 Heavy T.M. By.

WAR DIARY (contd.)
INTELLIGENCE SUMMARY
Army Form C. 2118

for Month of October

(Erase heading not required.)

Instructions regarding War Diaries and Intelligence Summaries are contained in F.S. Regs., Part II. and the Staff Manual respectively. Title Pages will be prepared in manuscript.

Place	Date	Hour	Summary of Events and Information	Remarks and references to Appendices
In the field 14th Oct.y (contd)	25.		Great activity in the rear. 15 A Frenchs exploded.	
			Range at R.E. Farm under 2 feet of water. Water from the whole hill appears to drain into this position.	
	26–31.		Further falls of earth at Antheme Road position, trenches still further retarded.	

J.M. Markworth
Lt. T.M.B
R.G.V 80 H.T.M. By.

War Diary.

of.

X 36 Trench Mortar
Battery.

for
October 1916.

Army Form C. 2118.

WAR DIARY
or
INTELLIGENCE SUMMARY
(Erase heading not required.)

X 36. T.M.B.

Place	Date	Hour	Summary of Events and Information	Remarks and references to Appendices
P.E. FARM	Oct 1st	6 P.M.	Enemy very quiet all day. No trench mortaring on our front or on either side. Battery on our right firing on own. Enemy not retaliating. We are still working on permanent position at Dead Cow's Farm. Weather is fine, and our aircraft very active. No artillery action.	
	Oct 2		No flying done on either side. Infantry raided last night, brought back a machine gun, helmets & rifles. To-day many of our grenades and German hand grenades are lying on parapet; also one of our legs injured rifles & two German rifles. Today we watched their men working at N 36 a 60, 30. It appears as if they are constructing something concrete. One man wore a steel helmet & the others wore caps.	
		6 a.m 3	Soon after 9.0 a.m. this morning T.M. batts, on our right started firing. The their MK1 & heavy T.Ms. into our sector in retaliation. On being retaliation with 30 bombs Stokes also fired a number of rounds & on about 11.0 a.m. we silenced the enemy mortars. Fired with T.M.S.O. to inspect of T.M. position by by Canadians near Piccadilly bench.	

2449 Wt. W14957/M90 750,000 1/16 J.B.C. & A. Forms/C.2118/12.

Army Form C. 2118.

WAR DIARY
or
INTELLIGENCE SUMMARY
(Erase heading not required.)

Instructions regarding War Diaries and Intelligence Summaries are contained in F. S. Regs., Part II. and the Staff Manual respectively. Title Pages will be prepared in manuscript.

Place	Date	Hour	Summary of Events and Information	Remarks and references to Appendices
R.E. Farm	4th Oct 1916		About 10 o'clock this morning the Bosch fired a few T.M. on our right & again at about 3 o'clock in the afternoon. Otto different times during the day he registered on the front line on the right of M. Sector with 15 c.m. strong. Put hole in old Canadian position near Piccadilly. The enemy gun hay also fire on D 4 from 7.30 p.m. till 8.45 p.m. on artillery retaliated. The Hun enemy own trenches between these times held out again. The trench mortars & rifle behind several hand grenades these crops rapid fire rifle & machine guns.	
	5th Oct 1916		From 8.30 a.m. it relieved till 9.35 a.m. there was a general T.M. strafe on the enemy line this morning. Of 9 gun on the right of Kingsway shot a formative its second round & blew both the pits in obliging one volunteer. Other 2 guns were in the old Canadian front line near Piccadilly & fired 37 rds. The shop was great for rest of day. The enemy did not alter 1 gun & wanted in its afternoon on new position great to left of Kingsway.	

WAR DIARY
or
INTELLIGENCE SUMMARY

(Erase heading not required.)

Army Form C. 2118.

Instructions regarding War Diaries and Intelligence Summaries are contained in F.S. Regs., Part II. and the Staff Manual respectively. Title Pages will be prepared in manuscript.

Place	Date	Hour	Summary of Events and Information	Remarks and references to Appendices
R.E. Farm	6th Nov 1916		Put shell in gun position for use in case of emergency. Commenced work on new position (attapos) just behind the one damaged yesterday in rigit of Ringing. Very quiet day.	
	7 Nov 1916		Working all day on new position. Received 6 wagon loads of material the evening. Had them dumped abreast of tramway.	
	8 Oct 1916		Carrying up material to dump near dug out. Working on new position. Got 2nd no 4 gun ready to fire by 7.20 p.m. Then saw O.C. 141st R.I. Rs received instructions to fire. Fired 27 rounds during gas attack 1.34 AM to 1.59 AM. Line very quiet all day, carried on digging positions.	
	9/10/16 1 am		Carried up ammunition a.o. day. Getting this gun in action. Front is quiet. No trench mortaring.	
	10/11/16 3pm			
	11/11/16 9 p.m		Saw the General's Group commander in the line now placed then around position. Fired 36 rounds in the afternoon in Support J.Y. 36. T.M.B. or 107th Bde or our night.	

Army Form C. 2118.

WAR DIARY
or
INTELLIGENCE SUMMARY
(Erase heading not required.)

Instructions regarding War Diaries and Intelligence Summaries are contained in F. S. Regs., Part II. and the Staff Manual respectively. Title Pages will be prepared in manuscript.

Place	Date	Hour	Summary of Events and Information	Remarks and references to Appendices
R.E. Farm	12/10/16		Got a working party of 2/H men from Artillery & carried on with permanent positions. Hun landed about 2 A.M. shelling which the enemy showed himself to have considerable artillery. Very quiet. Carried on with gun positions.	
	13/10/16			
	14/10/16	8.30 P.M.	Very quiet till 8.30 P.M. Enemy put over 4 T.M's. Retaliated quietened them down considerably. We fired 200 rounds in the dark, 2 mortars H.S. These were nearly delivered up plenty.	
	15/10/16		Working party of 12 men reported for work on permanent positions. Working party of 12 men reported for work on permanent positions at Battery & Piccadilly given Fired 16 rnds in retaliation 38 rnds in reply of Y Battery.	
	16/10/16		Working party as above. Fired 30 rnds in morning on Boche front wire retaliation. In the afternoon the Boche put over 6 & we replied with 15. Sent Stokes gun to S.O.M. Scheme. Working party as above. Fired 150 rounds from S.A.C. Fired 107 rnds in staff Boche retaliation. Quiet morning. During staff on rifle mechanism blew out 2 gun. Received 100 bombs from S.A.C. Sent to S.O.M. adm. live duds gun out.	
	17-10-16			

Army Form C. 2118.

WAR DIARY
or
INTELLIGENCE SUMMARY
(Erase heading not required.)

Place	Date	Hour	Summary of Events and Information	Remarks and references to Appendices
R.E. Farm	18-10-16		Working party as above, also 10 men from S.A.C. engaged in carrying hurdles. Quiet day. Engaged in repairing huts. In aft. enemy fired 3 rnds for purpose of testing their Boche did not reply.	
	19-10-16		Artillery working party reported as usual. Full scale shown back as it were. Raining hard & no work could be done on positions. Very quiet all day.	
	20-10-16		10mm fire. Heavy T.M.B. reported for work on permanent positions, this to be at unknown shell hole & open position as they never considered old fallen in as a result of yesterdays rain. Starts digging new position just below S.W. whole ground very wet. Have two holes in open.	
	21-10-16		10 men from Heavy T.M.B. reported for work on permanent positions, also 8 men from artillery who were on carrying up material. Find their men positions in they yesterday has fallen in today.	
	22nd		Very quiet all day, party gone to new position, working party 10 men from ½ Coy to enter permanent position with working party, 10 men from ½ Coy. on reinstatement permanent position with all Aircraft active. 1-36 T.M.B. 90 rnds enemy fire at all.	

Army Form C. 2118.

WAR DIARY
or
INTELLIGENCE SUMMARY
(Erase heading not required.)

Instructions regarding War Diaries and Intelligence Summaries are contained in F. S. Regs., Part II. and the Staff Manual respectively. Title Pages will be prepared in manuscript.

Place	Date	Hour	Summary of Events and Information	Remarks and references to Appendices
RE Farm	23/10/16	6pm	Carried on with permanent emplacement; enemy fired on 1.5 minenwerfers doing little damage. Retaliated with TB. Bombs effectively silencing the enemy.	
	24/10/16		Very quiet, & no firing done on either side	
	25/10/16		Enemy put 18 minenwerfers on our area, doing no damage. Retaliated with TB bombs, silencing him for today. Bombs had good effect	
	26/10/16		Enemy active. Put over 40 heavy & light minenwerfers, doing some damage. Retaliated with 127. Carried on with permanent positions.	
	27/10/16		Quiet all day. No firing. Carried on with permanent positions. Weather very windy & rainy.	
	28/10/16		Quiet no firing. Sappers carried on with permanent positions. 10 D.A.C. men carried up stores to prevent positions Very Quiet.	
	29-10-16			

Army Form C. 2118.

WAR DIARY
or
INTELLIGENCE SUMMARY
(Erase heading not required.)

Instructions regarding War Diaries and Intelligence Summaries are contained in F. S. Regs., Part II. and the Staff Manual respectively. Title Pages will be prepared in manuscript.

Place	Date	Hour	Summary of Events and Information	Remarks and references to Appendices
R.E. Farm	30-10-16		Between 12.30 & 12.45 p.m. Bosche put over one heavy & one lighter T.M. & retaliated with 17 bombs. Work progressing with movement operations.	
	31-10-16		Quite day nothing. Preparing for tonight's raid. Also put shot on twenty-five 18 pdr shrapnel for purpose of cutting wire. No movement as normal.	
	1-11-16		12.15 to 4.15 a.m. Fired during raid 68 bombs stokes + 18 relating with a few rounds 18 pdr shrapnel + lighter T.M.	

J.C. MacCallumdel 7 pdr
O.C. X 367 T.M.B.

Army Form C. 2118

WAR DIARY
INTELLIGENCE SUMMARY
(Erase heading not required.)

1/36th Trench Mortar Battery.

Place	Date Oct '16	Hour	Summary of Events and Information	Remarks and references to Appendices
In the line	2		We fired 60 rounds on enemy's wire & trenches. Heavy retaliation with heavy & Medium Minenwerfer & two light T.M.	
	3		Receives orders from Group Commander to take 2 guns out of action & send them back to billets. Just after guns were removed enemy was very active with his T.M's — heavy, medium & light — for about ½ an hour. Two casualties to our equipment or personnel.	
	4		Took one gun back & registered with two rounds on were at N.36.D.29.70. Soon after getting back had left. Medium retaliation vigorously with T.M's & rifle grenades.	
	5		During bombardment of our front & fire minutes (from 6.30 to 9.35 a.m.) we fired 44 rounds in front 14 minutes & cut enemy's wire well. The Men was hot. Open fire for 10 minutes, his retaliation very heavy during second & last firings of the bombardment.	
	6		The G.O.C., R.A., & Group Commander inspected & approved of new positions & one in course of construction.	
	7		Quiet day. Made progress with work on spring back position.	
	9		Commenced work & got on well with 3 new temporary positions. Fired 24 rounds on to Cudmore Farm during the afternoon. Enemy retaliated with from	

Army Form C. 2118

WAR DIARY
or
INTELLIGENCE SUMMARY
(Erase heading not required.)

Place	Date	Hour	Summary of Events and Information	Remarks and references to Appendices
Juttielies	9 cont'd		20 to 30 "pip-squeaks" & heavy shells slung back & vicinity with T.M.G.	
	10		Completes 3 temporary positions & places 50 rounds ammo at each gun position. Took up guns to 3 temporary positions & after registration fired 39 rounds. The Boche replying with 16 Minenwerfer, one of which unusually unmasked at Hayto & slightly wounded Cpl. Wareham.	
	11			
	12		Took No 1 gun we fired 40 rounds on Morton Farm, commencing at 2 am. A quarter of an hour later we opened with the two other guns, their firing 15 rounds in five minutes. No 3 gun received a Direct hit from a Minenwerfer which wounded Cpl. Kerman, Privates Knott & Schiller, the latter receiving also a foot. Later on the Sergeant working in positions for new Dug-outs & trenches No 3 gun which has been hastily dismantled.	
	13		We opened a very say carrying ammunition to Bryces Farm & work on positions	
	15		Guns 2 guns in N 36 D opens fire on enemy's wire, expending altogether 99 rounds. The wind was bad against adequate shooting. At Bryles Farm we fired a further 40 rounds in registration & an endeavour to knock out a M.G. -emplacement.	
	16		At 3:30 pm we opened fire on several widely cut & good lanes though were at N 36 D 40.30, expending 20 rounds. The Boche sent over small Minenwerfer in retaliation	

WAR DIARY or INTELLIGENCE SUMMARY

Army Form C. 2118

Place	Date	Hour	Summary of Events and Information	Remarks and references to Appendices
In trenches 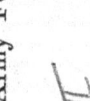	17		Fires with 2 guns as were at T6B 90.90. We got rid of No 1 gun and No 2 gun J.H.5 with No 2 gun, both finally going out of action. Both No 1 gun the rifle mechanism flew out of the adapter & with No 2 gun the whole gas & spring slipped backwards & went through the roof of the trench during the "strafe". The strain was all weights of shells, no casualties.	
	18 19 20 21 22		We worked on new temporary positions, being 20 yards on the 20th by town of V.36 Bty. These were attached to V.36 Bty on the 22nd. Very wet weather on 18th & 19th.	
	23		Commencing at 2 p.m. we fired 6 rounds in registration on west at V1A 27.68 & then the gun was put out of action through the rifle mechanism blowing out & stripping threads of adapter. The bombs exploded in Boyles farm with one Minenwerfer of about 10 M.m. shells. We also fired 6 rounds from No 1 & 2 gun in retaliation to several light T.M.'s fire west Durham Road. We fired 15 rounds from Boyles farm on west were at V1A 27.66 & 60 rounds from No 1 & 2 guns in trenches from N36R 65.15 to 75.00. Boyles farm & No 1 gun put out of action through rifle mechanism blowing out. Gun firing	
	24		Lasted from 2.30 to 3.30 p.m.	
	26		Placed two guns in new positions N 36 C & fired fire with both at 5 p.m. on west from N 36 D 15.90, 20.15 & 35.66. Rifle mechanism flew out of No 1 gun	

WAR DIARY

INTELLIGENCE SUMMARY
(Erase heading not required.)

Army Form C. 2118

IV

Place	Date	Hour	Summary of Events and Information	Remarks and references to Appendices
In the Field	26 Cont		After 2nd rounds 1 one of No 2 gun at 75th rounds, both a/aplus keeping being stripped of guns put out of action. From 3.6 H.pm. we fired 40 rounds from Boyles Farm on new at U/A 27.66. The Bosche retaliating with about 10 Minenwerfers, numerous light T.M's & 77 mm. shells.	
	28		Opened fire at 2pm. from Boyles Farm on enemy's wire, expending 14 rounds, H.E. which fell very short. The Boche replies with 3" Minenwerfers, several light T.M's & numerous 77 mm. shells.	
	30		From 12 noon to 12.45 we fired 30 rounds from Boyles Farm on new at U/A 27.66 & with No 3 gun set rounds on N 36 d 20.75. In retaliation the Hun fired my eight Minenwerfers both right of Boyles Farm, several light T.M's & 77 mm on Boyles Farm & one Minenwerfer & several light T.M's on on T 6 3	
	31.		Quiet day, working on positions	

J A Price Lt-R.F.A.
Comm'g Y 36 T.M. Bty.

Army Form C. 2118

WAR DIARY for October
or
INTELLIGENCE SUMMARY Z/36 Trench Mortar Battery
(Erase heading not required.)

Instructions regarding War Diaries and Intelligence Summaries are contained in F.S. Regs., Part II. and the Staff Manual respectively. Title Pages will be prepared in manuscript.

Place	Date	Hour	Summary of Events and Information	Remarks and references to Appendices
In the Field	1-10-16		Preparing temporary position at Boyles Farm – Situation quiet. Nothing to report.	DHH
	2-10-16		Action from temporary position at Boyles Farm. 2 guns fired 50 rounds at around Ontario Farm. U.1.A 50.70. Very little retaliation from enemy.	DHH
	3-10-16		Work on temporary gun emplacements at charred stakes position near Dairy Post – Situation quiet.	DHH
	4-10-16		Completion of work on these temporary positions for shoot on following day – Situation quiet.	DHH
	5-10-16		Got into action at 8.30 a.m. & fired 61 rounds – very little retaliation. No casualties to report.	DHH
	6-10-16		Work carried out on temporary position at Boyles Farm – necessary for bom bombardment the following day. Situation quiet.	DHH

Army Form C. 2118

Instructions regarding War Diaries and Intelligence
Summaries are contained in F.S. Regs., Part II.
and the Staff Manual respectively. Title Pages
will be prepared in manuscript.

WAR DIARY for October
or
INTELLIGENCE SUMMARY
(Erase heading not required.)

Place	Date	Hour	Summary of Events and Information	Remarks and references to Appendices
In the Field	7-10-16		In action at Boyles Farm with 2 guns at 4 o'clock p.m. 32 Rounds were fired – Very little retaliation from enemy. No casualties to report.	LgHu
	8-10-16		Preparation of temporary positions near the Osiers for completion on the 11th. Situation quiet.	LgHu
	9-10-16		Work on temporary positions. Situation quiet.	LgHu BrHu
	10-10-16		Work on temporary positions. Situation quiet.	LgHu
	12-10-16		In action from temporary positions – 2 guns – 2-8 a.m. Fired 17 Rounds (Raid). Very little retaliation from enemy. Gnr Hayes No 35894 – Severely wounded depressed fracture of skull.	LgHu
	13-10-16		In action at 7-30 a.m. Retaliation. No casualties to report. Work carried out to temporary positions at U.1.d.9.8 & U.1.d.9.2-5.0.	LgHu
	14-10-16		In action at 11-0 a.m. from these temporary positions with 2 guns. 105 Rounds fired. No casualties to report.	LgHu

1875 Wt. W593/826 1,000,000 4/15 J.B.C. & A. A.D.S.S./Forms/C. 2118.

Army Form C. 2118

WAR DIARY for October
or
INTELLIGENCE SUMMARY
(Erase heading not required.)

Instructions regarding War Diaries and Intelligence Summaries are contained in F.S. Regs., Part II. and the Staff Manual respectively. Title Pages will be prepared in manuscript.

Place	Date	Hour	Summary of Events and Information	Remarks and references to Appendices
In the Field	15-10-16		Prepared temporary positions near Orion Bees. Situation quiet	
	16-10-16		Registered 2 rounds on target U.2.a. 80.20 Completed work to positions. No enemy retaliation. Situation quiet.	
	17-10-16		Got into action at 4 p.m. with two guns & fired 23 rounds. - Both guns put out of action. Heavy retaliation. No casualties.	
	18-10-16		Work on temporary positions + D.A.C. men at work on dug outs. Situation quiet.	
	19-10-16		In action with 2 guns at 11 a.m. from temporary positions. Fired 43 Bombs Very little enemy retaliation. V Battery men at work on dug outs.	
	20-10-16		Preparing temporary positions also work on dug outs. Situation quiet.	
	21-10-16		In action at 3 p.m. with two guns & fired 79 rounds. Slight enemy retaliation. No casualties. V Battery men & D.A.C. men at work on dug outs.	
	22-10-16		Work on dug outs. Situation quiet.	

Army Form C. 2118

WAR DIARY for October
or
INTELLIGENCE SUMMARY
(Erase heading not required.)

Instructions regarding War Diaries and Intelligence Summaries are contained in F. S. Regs., Part II. and the Staff Manual respectively. Title Pages will be prepared in manuscript.

Place	Date	Hour	Summary of Events and Information	Remarks and references to Appendices
In the Field	23-10-16		Preparation of temporary positions & work on dug outs. Situation quiet	23[?]
	24-10-16		Work on temporary positions & dug outs. Situation quiet.	23[?]
	25-10-16		Two guns in action at 11 a.m. from temporary positions. Employed on enemy Bomb Store. Fired 106 rounds. Heavy enemy retaliation. No casualties to report.	18[?]
	26-10-16		Preparation of temporary positions. V Battery work on dug outs. Situation quiet	29[?]
	27-10-16		Work on temporary positions & V Battery work on dug out. Situation quiet.	22[?]
	28-10-16		In action with 2 guns from temporary positions at 11-30 a.m. Fired 62 Rounds. Very little enemy retaliation. No casualties. V Battery men at work on dug out.	19[?]
	29-10-16		Work on temporary positions & new dug out. Situation quiet.	29[?]
	30-10-16		Temporary gun positions repaired & a new one started. Work on dug out.	19[?]
	31-10-16		Work carried out on new temporary positions also on dug out. Situation quiet	19[?]

J. J. Ward. Lt Col. R.F.A.
Comdg 177 Bde R.F.A.

Fourteen

WAR DIARY
INTELLIGENCE SUMMARY
(Erase heading not required.)

November 1916 — Army Form C. 2118

36 Divisional T. Mortar Batt?

V of 4

Place	Date	Hour	Summary of Events and Information	Remarks and references to Appendices
R.E. Farm	1/11/16	4.25 a.m.	L Battery fired during Infantry Raid 68 bombs. Enemy retaliated with a few whizz bangs. Slight T.M.s.	
		2.15 p.m.	R Battery fired 84 bombs cutting wire between N36 A 56-62 and N36 A 56/80. Enemy retaliated with 20 T.M.s and a few light shells.	
	2/11/16	11.30 a.m.	Z Battery fired 100 rounds target U 2 a. 10.12. Enemy Rn a few medium shells U 1 d. 80.10.	
	3/11/16	3 p.m.	Y Battery fired 81 bombs in conjunction with Stokes on N 36 d 15790 to N 36 d 35/68. Two very short rounds from No 4 gun attributed to bad charges. Enemy retaliated with Minnies 10.5 & 7.7 along our front.	
		3.30 p.m.	X Battery fired 55 rounds on N 36 a 80/25 and N 36 a 70.35. No enemy T.M. retaliation, but a number of 7.7 cm air bursts. Enemy artillery were active on all sectors chiefly 10.5 & 7.7 cm.	
	4/11/16	3 p.m.	X Battery fired 69 rounds on N 36 a 55/80 to 3/52. Slight retaliation. The Battery was congratulated on the bombardment by Corps Commander who watched the shoot from Kemmel Hill.	
		10 a.m.	Z fired 40 rounds on U 2 b. 3/3. Retaliation 10.5 & 7.7 cm.	
		3.15 p.m.	A few enemy T.M. were fired into the centre sector and Y Battery replied with 4 bombs, but did not continue firing as the Infantry were carrying out a relief.	

WAR DIARY — November 1916 — Army Form C. 2118

INTELLIGENCE SUMMARY — 36 Divisional T Mortar Batt^s

(Erase heading not required.)

Place	Date	Hour	Summary of Events and Information	Remarks and references to Appendices
	5/11/16		Weather bad, no firing. All Batteries worked on their positions.	
	6/11/16			
	5/11/16	2.30pm	Heavy Battery fired 5 rounds from their R.E. farm position.	
	7/11/16	4p.m	X Battery fired 40 rounds target N36 a 9.0.4.0. in reply to enemy trench mortaring.	
		3p.m	Y Battery fired 82 rounds at mortar farm. Enemy replied with 12. 7.7 cm. on position at 3.20. and again at 3.45 with 30 more. Shoot was very successful many direct hits on trench mortar dug outs being observed.	
	8/11/16		During bad weather much trouble was experienced with positions, work was carried on draining & improving.	
	12/11/16			
	12/11/16	2p.m	L Battery fired 22 rounds on wire at N 30 c. 52.15 hot retaliation.	
	13/11/16	2p.m	L Battery fired 76 rounds & reed wire from N36 a 52.98 to N30 c 43.30. This wire was all mended by the enemy during the night.	
	14/11/16	2.30pm	Q Battery fired 24 rounds recutting gaps in mended wire: no enemy retaliation.	
	15/11/16	11.30am	In accordance with O.O. No 16. L fired 122 rounds Y 146 rounds and Z 182 rounds. Mortars were covered by Stokes trench and enemy retaliation was slight. V Heavy Battery fired 23 rounds from its Gootzebern farm emplacement & 20 rounds from its Gootzebern farm emplacement.	

- 3 -

Army Form C. 2118

WAR DIARY
or
INTELLIGENCE SUMMARY
(Erase heading not required.)

Month: November 1916
Unit: 36 Divisional T. Mortar Batty

Place	Date	Hour	Summary of Events and Information	Remarks and references to Appendices
	16/11/16	10 p.m	R. fired 121 rounds at M.G. emplacement during Infantry Raid by 9th Innskillings. These rounds were fired by silence but 3 rounds dropped short, so silence was abandoned. Screen about 8 ft high made a good protection. mortars firing with artillery.	
	17/11/16	10.15 a.m.	Y Battery fired 763 rounds on the centre sector considerable damage was done to the enemy's line. L Battery fired 35 rounds at a M.G. position from S.9. Several hits were secured. The bombs failed to damage the concrete.	
	18/11/16		R Battery fires 25 rounds in reply to 2 enemy T. Mortars. Z Battery fired 2 rounds at U.2 & 6/9 to test Temple silencer. Series was stopped by the gun check of silencer turning in the bore.	
	19/11/16	8.30 a.m.	Y Battery fired 7 rounds with silencer. The 7th round fell behind front line. Later in the day another 10 rounds were fired, in reply to enemy T mortars, without silencer and one round was again about 75 yards was well.	
		2.30 p.m.	X Battery fired 700 rounds in reply to T2. Enemy T.M. Considerable damage was done to enemy's line & hostile mortar was silenced.	
	20th to 23		All Batteries were busy preparing temporary positions for a combined bombardment on the 23.	
	23	11.30	Combined Heavy Artillery, flight T.M. bombardment. Enemy retaliated with 7.7 & 10 cm a few T. Mortars. The shoot was very successful enemy trenches being obliterated. V. Fired 33 rounds at 328 Y. 200 and Z 179. Target N36a 53/78 to 62/47	

4

Army Form C. 2118

November 1916

Tom Fleet

WAR DIARY
or
INTELLIGENCE SUMMARY 36 Divisional Trench Mortar Battery

(Erase heading not required.)

Instructions regarding War Diaries and Intelligence Summaries are contained in F.S. Regs., Part II. and the Staff Manual respectively. Title Pages will be prepared in manuscript.

Place	Date	Hour	Summary of Events and Information	Remarks and references to Appendices
	24/11/16	10.30 a.m.	Z Battery fired 48 rounds with 4 + 16 rounds without Temple silence on enemy newwork in U 2 a and U 2 c. Enemy retaliation slight	
	25/11/16	10 a.m.	Y fired 5 rounds with silence and 4 without silence, several rounds were short so % ceased fire	
		11 a.m.	X fired 98 rounds with Temple silence. Very successful shoot on U/2a & U/2c. Enemy did not retaliate	
	26/11/16	2.45 pm	Y fired 7 rounds with silence. 2 rolled back – fire (gun) was ceased. The charges were believed to be damp.	
	27/11/16	3 p.m.	X fired 16 rounds with Temple silence. Satisfactory	
	28/11/16		Batteries 2" preparing for combined bombardment.	
	29/11/16		Bombardment postponed.	
	30/11/16	2 p.m.	Combined bombardment with medium + light mortars on Lentz sector. X fired 350 rounds. Y 210 and Z 250. Much damage was done to the enemy trenches mm. The mortars were well served under a rather heavy retaliation with 4.2's and 3" during the month the Heavy Battery fired 81 rounds (2 guns only) and the 2" Mortars fired 3449. E. 1536, 7998 and J. 915. This was in spite of the fact that the heavy rains seriously hampered operations. This amount of ammunition represents a weight of nearly 100 tons.	

.... Capt. R.F.A.
T.M.S.O. 36th Div. Arty.

WAR DIARY
INTELLIGENCE SUMMARY

Army Form C. 2118.

Place	Date Dec	Hour	Summary of Events and Information	Remarks and references to Appendices
In the woods	2		Y 36 Bty tested Temple Silencer, successfully firing 2 rounds. A third round dropped before one front lines, so the test was deferred. J 36 Bty also tested with Temple Silencer, also Silencer on V2C 60.90, many camouflaged screen for drawing flash.	
	3		A further test of Temple Silencer was made by Y 36 Bty who fired 20 rounds from front line.	
	4		Twenty-two rounds were expended by X 36 Bty, 7 to test screen for hiding flash. Enemy retaliated with 10 heavy trench mortars. Y 36 Bty again tested Temple Silenced with 18 rounds, also flash screen with two X 36 Bty houses were all positions to 16th Division. J 36 Bty fired 161 rounds from temporary position on V2A 20.20 to V2C 90.60. 7.	
	5		X 36 Bty returns Y 35 Bty of two positions near Curlu. Same tested at Irefull Farm.	
	6		In the morning Y 36 fired 94 rounds to the afternoon, in co-operation with the Stokes mortars, a further 23, two German mortars being active.	
	7		Ninety-two rounds were expended by Y 36, the same two enemy TMs being active as the previous day.	

WAR DIARY
INTELLIGENCE SUMMARY

(Erase heading not required.)

Army Form C. 2118.

Place	Date	Hour	Summary of Events and Information	Remarks and references to Appendices
In the field	13		V 36 Heavy Bty registered on U.8.B. 40.45 with gun at Gooseberry Farm firing 3 rounds; also registering on J.8.B 09.88 with gun in temporary position at Grab Farm (two rounds) & the enemy's stores.	
	15		V 36 Heavy Bty's gun at Gooseberry Farm fires 13 rounds on enemy support line at V.8.R 30 to G.O.B 347 21. The Grab Farm gun fires 12 rounds on enemy support line at U.8.R 09.88. There was considerable movement in the enemy's lines, probably due to the heavy storm of the previous day.	

Army Form C. 2118.

WAR DIARY
or
INTELLIGENCE SUMMARY

(Erase heading not required.)

Instructions regarding War Diaries and Intelligence Summaries are contained in F.S. Regs., Part II. and the Staff Manual respectively. Title Pages will be prepared in manuscript.

Place	Date Dec	Hour	Summary of Events and Information	Remarks and references to Appendices
In the Trenches	8		Registration at Antoni's Farm was carried out by X.36. Y Bty took part in a bombardment & got 1 of 56 127 rounds ; retaliation heavy. X.36 registered a gun in Cluwcroft Avenue.	
	9		J Bty covered by artillery, fired 64 rounds on U.2.C.70.60. Hostile fire being heavy the Boche threw out 9 TMs & was kept down with his artillery from 11.30 to 2.30 p.m. Y Bty replying with 32 rounds on Mortar Dam.	
	11		Our snipers the Boche put three "oil-cans" into Antoni's Farm. Y Bty effectively silenced with 6 bombs from X.36. ✗ See Doku 1.A. For 13th Dec	
	13		In a counterattack X Bty with three guns discharged 112 rounds with good effect. Y Bty from 3 guns in Walker Trench put rounds round & Portile dune from U.8.C.15.17 to U.8.B.00.33. Simultaneously J Bty fired 52 rounds on Le Petite Douve Dam. Retaliation very heavy, one N.CO. wounded & 2 gunners killed. ✗ See Doku 1.A. For Remarks Re 15th Dec	
	15		Y Bty fired 60 rounds on Mortar Dam in retaliation to hostile T.Ms. 2 French R.A. Marshall Austinies "shell shock" in this stink. X Bty gave the Boche 15" rounds for two; & Y.36 sent 46 over N.36.B.15.80. 31 rounds in retaliation	
	18.			

WAR DIARY
INTELLIGENCE SUMMARY

(Erase heading not required.)

Army Form C. 2118.

Place	Date	Hour	Summary of Events and Information	Remarks and references to Appendices
In the trenches	23		When gas was sent over from Center Sector enemy shelled Lesboeufs area.	
	25		At 3.45 p.m. the boche vigorously bombards, with his guns and howitzers, the front area of 426 Bty but no reply was given. T.M's 3 Bty got 6" Trench Mortar into action for the first time & discharged 80 rounds. The Huns' retaliation being both heavy & accurate.	
	26		Hostile artillery damages 6-inch position being hurt by Y Bty who fires 6 bursts in reply to three Minnenwerfer	
	27		6" Mortar to new position	
	28		With good results 3 Bty fires 90 rounds from 6-inch Mortar, the enemy retaliation being fairly heavy. 3 Bty removes	

A.........
Capt, R.F.A.
T.M.S.O. 36th Div. Arty.

WAR DIARY
INTELLIGENCE SUMMARY
(Erase heading not required.)

Army Form C. 2118.

Vol B

36 Divisional Trench Mortar Batteries

Place	Date	Hour	Summary of Events and Information	Remarks and references to Appendices
In the field	Jany 1917 2		X 36 Bty fired 106 rounds of 2" ammunition in bombardment on 107th Bde front & 37 rounds from 6" Stokes mortar featuring two canisters (NCO i/cm wounded) in 6" detachment. Y 36 Bty came into action opposite to a tree at Portken. Ammunition with 2" mortar. 3.36 Bty tetachments to two small Howitzers with 2 guns. Y 36 Bty fires 9 Jany 35 from Durham Road Trench on Hostile support line N 36 D 90.45 to 97.35. 2nd round hostiles by bombs. One round of concrete or ? firing the guns one to concussion.	
	3		During the morning X Bty took over Y Bty's position on 107 Bde front. X Bty fires gun tested in retaliation. Twelve rounds were fired by 3 Bty from gun in Crater South of U 2 A 20.20 in reply to small trench mortars.	
	6		2/Lt Brown in command in temp. absence of Lt Angus by X Bty. He 6 shots were fired in retaliation by 3 Bty to R.B.G. 2nd am the tenth rates MGs at Durban Road.	
	8		Y 36 Heavy Bty were engaged in searching out & camouflaging information at Durban Road. Retaliation to enemy TM fire was made by X Bty who fired 10 rounds.	

Army Form C. 2118.

WAR DIARY
or
INTELLIGENCE SUMMARY.
(Erase heading not required.)

Army Troops 36 Division 1 French Mortar Battery

Place	Date	Hour	Summary of Events and Information	Remarks and references to Appendices
In the field	July 1917 9		Another 35 rounds were discharged by X Bty in reply to enemy fire	
	10		39 on the following day	
	11		Y Bty took over position from X Bty who moved to hostile spur in that	
	12		In the afternoon and engaged; but Y Bty's high position also showed as a target; one of the Bty's guns was wrecked, no damage done. Two direct hits with 77 mm shells were made on trench leading to Y Bty's Durham Road gun	
	16		There was interrmittent shelling with 77 mm and 10 cm shells. Several of them on the Y Bty's high position slightly damaging the roof of new front store. Y Bty's Durham Road trenches were shelled with 77 mm H.E. shrapnel & 10 cm. H.E. and one hit, two 77 mm fracing within 2 feet of the lip of the wall. The Boche scored two direct H.E. hits on the centre dug-out of Y Bty but no impression was made. There was the fourth time this dug-out has been hit.	
	19		3 Bty handed over to X Bty prior to proceeding to Bethem for a rest	
	20		Z Bty just after taking over, fired 15 rounds so in retaliation	

WAR DIARY or INTELLIGENCE SUMMARY.

Army Form C. 2118.

26 Divisional T.M. Batteries

Place	Date	Hour	Summary of Events and Information	Remarks and references to Appendices
In the field	January 1917 22		Enemy T.M's were very active on 16th Division front, & in reply & about 10 light bombs on enemy trench N 36.d. Y.Bty fired 30 rounds. The enemy's X Bty was heavily bombarded in the afternoon. This Bty was out of 35 rounds & had all their rifle mechanism sent out of action. The detachments were withdrawn & home rifle mechanism sent for. In the meantime the enemy fired 8 & took gun from Antons came. During the day X Bty fired by V.Bty were cancelled, one man being hit trying to rescue the ammunition. Enemy Batteries were very unsatisfactory. Owing to fog & smoke it was impossible, whilst work at enemy gun positions in flashes was held up by lack of material & difficulty of getting it forward.	
	23-31			
	24		At 3.30 pm an enemy battery shelled Y Bty premises & set to stand-to. Several rifle grenades, The Bty stood to, but was not required to fire.	
	25		Enemy aeroplanes were very active & one in particular flew very low over Y Bty & dropped bombs.	
	26		There was much activity with front of aircraft on the 1 following days. Otherwise the situation was quiet.	

WAR DIARY or INTELLIGENCE SUMMARY.

Army Form C. 2118.

(Erase heading not required.)

36 Divisional T.M. Batteries

Place	Date	Hour	Summary of Events and Information	Remarks and references to Appendices
Sillylecul	Jany 1917 28		Z Bty on return from rest camp relieved Y Bty at R.E. tram pushing S fires 20 rounds in retaliation. X Bty started to construct T.M. gunhouse positions. V Bty under orders from left Group withdraw their heavy mortar from Durham Road.	
	29		X Bty fired 35 rounds at enemy wire. V Bty withdrew mortar from Grandcourt dump under orders from right Group to B.L. Reserves. A direct hit on V Bty's ammunition near turning at Durham Road. It shell — probably 10 c.m. with delay action fuse — penetrating concrete roofing of 3 ft of frozen earth, smashing 6 H.E. bombs and 5 explosive ones.	
	30		Defensive fire tasks were completed by X Bty 6.50 rounds were carried to each.	

J.H. Gulyan.. Capt, R.F.A.
T.M.S.O. 38th Div. Arty.

Army Form C. 2118.

WAR DIARY
or
INTELLIGENCE SUMMARY.
(Erase heading not required.)

36 Div: Arty. T.M. Batteries
February 1917.

Instructions regarding War Diaries and Intelligence Summaries are contained in F. S. Regs., Part II. and the Staff Manual respectively. Title pages will be prepared in manuscript.

Place	Date	Hour	Summary of Events and Information	Remarks and references to Appendices
In trenches	1/2/17	12.c	X36 Bty. fired 20 rounds for the purpose of wire cutting from position at Anton's dam. Z36 fires on N36 D 80.40 as punishment for small enemy T.M's. Work in hands by V36 at Durham Roads held up owing to frost. X36 cut wire at Seaforth dam, expending 114 rounds. All other work held up owing to frost.	
	2		Wire was cut at Anton's dam by X36 who discharged 22 rounds. Z36 fires 34 rounds on N36 D 80.30 & 80.50; enemy's retaliation was feeble.	
	3		With an expenditure of 30 rounds X36 cut wire opposite Seaforth dam. L Right Group bombardment of enemy wire X36 firing 60 rounds, 30 from Seaforth dam & 30 from Anton's dam. Z36 fires 25 rounds as punishment for heavy enemy T.M's on N36 D 80.50 & 80.40. V36 restarts work at Durham Roads, but progress was slow owing to frost & lack of material.	
	4			
	5			
	6		More wire was cut by X36 at U 15 A 26.96, ten rounds being fired. Y36 completes defence positions on Hill 63.	
	8		Further wire cutting was carried out by X36 at U & B 20.18 with 26 rounds.	

WAR DIARY
or
INTELLIGENCE SUMMARY

Army Form C. 2118.

Place	Date	Hour	Summary of Events and Information	Remarks and references to Appendices
L Hotois & Contn	July 1914			
	9		A gun was put in action by Y.36 at Antoni Farm. L. Right Group bombardment X Bty fires with two guns 33 rounds on U9C 10.38. Z.36 fires 42 rounds on enemy's lines N.36 D 70.40 & 30.40 & also bombards hostile trenches from Antoni Farm to U15 A 30.60 to 30.90. Y.36 fires 9 rounds from Antoni Farm in left Group operations on Communication trenches U9C 54.56 to U9C 10.30	
	10		X.36 were relieved in the line by Y.36. Z.36 fires 32 rounds in retaliation to medium & heavy hostile T.M's on N.36 D 50.70. X.36 commences rest training at billets in Hene Eglise. Y.36 fires 20 rounds at wire north of Ulrica Sap U15 A 2.9 & Z.36 fires 30 rounds on N.36 D 60.30 & 60.40, drawing only slight retaliation from the enemy.	
	11		Thirty rounds were fires by Y.36 from Seaforth Farm on wire to the right of Avenue Farm & 10 rounds were sent over on Ulrica Sap from a gun in the front line. Z.36 expends 40 rounds on N.36 D 70.30 & the enemy's retaliation was with medium T.M's.	
	12.			

Army Form C. 2118.

WAR DIARY
or
INTELLIGENCE SUMMARY.
(Erase heading not required.)

Instructions regarding War Diaries and Intelligence Summaries are contained in F.S. Regs., Part II. and the Staff Manual respectively. Title pages will be prepared in manuscript.

Place	Date	Hour	Summary of Events and Information	Remarks and references to Appendices
St Ingles	July '14 13		Y36 fires Antoni Farm gun on wire at Ulrica Sap, expending 30 rounds, & Z36 sent over 75 rounds on enemy line N36 D 70.30 & 60.40. The Boche retaliates with heavy & light T.M's.	
	14		Iron gun at fearful Farm discharges 30 rounds on wire to the right of Avenue Farm, whilst Z36 drops 35 rounds in the enemy's line N36 D 60.40 – 70.20.	
	15		In retaliation to hostile fire Y36 expent over 36 rounds amongst. He were at U9C 15.15 & U9C 4.1 & Z36 got totals of 42 rounds on N36 D 60.30, 60.40 & 70.20, meeting with only slight retaliation. Thirty rounds were fired by Y36 on wire at Ulrica Sap, the Boche replying with four "oil-cans." Z36's expenditure for the day was 24 rounds.	
	16		Y36 sent over 9 rounds at 11 a.m. from Antoni Farm during a bombardment of daylight raids by the 25th Division. This Battery was out of action from 11.30 to 5 p.m. owing to half-a-dozen rifle mechanisms going out of order.	
	17		In reply to 40 rounds on N36 D 70.30 & 70.40 by Z36 the Boche sent over a liberal supply of heavy & medium T.M's.	

WAR DIARY
or
INTELLIGENCE SUMMARY.
(Erase heading not required.)

Army Form C. 2118.

Place	Date	Hour	Summary of Events and Information	Remarks and references to Appendices
Dickebush	July/'14 18		X Bty on relieving Z Bty in left sector fires 37 rounds in retaliation. One gun team were taken by Y36 to fire 24 rounds through rifle mechanism becoming defective.	
	19		Kept training was begun by Z 36 at house Eglise billets. X Bty fires 11 rounds in retaliation; Y36 sent over 26 rounds in the wire to the Left of Ulrica Sap & V 36 put a gun in action at Durham Road.	
	20		X 36 fires two guns in bombardment, expending 37 rounds. Y Bty fires on wire at U 15 B 25.88 from Antonio dam & 41 rounds during bombardment south of Mortal dam. V Bty fires 15 rounds of heavy T.M. ammunition, enfilading Nutmeg Avenue Communication trench, N 36 B 84.65 — O 3 C 21.72.	
	21		Y Bty fires 6 rounds with Temple Silences in registration & at 7.30 pm bombards (with four guns) enemy's line, getting off 14 rounds with the silences.	
	22.		Like the previous day it was very misty, but X Bty dislodges 24 rounds (12 with silences) from our front line. Y 36 shoots 6 at 5.30 a.m.	

Army Form C. 2118.

WAR DIARY
or
INTELLIGENCE SUMMARY.
(Erase heading not required.)

Place	Date	Hour	Summary of Events and Information	Remarks and references to Appendices
In the trenches	July 14 22 Contd		owing to a heavy bombardment by the Boche & a raid on the New Zealanders' front. Eighty rounds were discharges by X Bty on enemy front line & were with good effect.	
	23	At 11.30 a.m. X Bty fires 32 rounds on wire in Red Avenue. X Bty expends 48 rounds on enemy front line, eight with the	
	24		Silencer. Y 36 commences a week's training at Hevre Eglise rear billets, having been relieved by Z Battery.	
	25			

.... Capt. F.F.A.
T.M.S.O. 38th Div. Arty.

Army Form C. 2118.

WAR DIARY
or
INTELLIGENCE SUMMARY. 36th Div. Artillery, T.M. Batteries

(Erase heading not required.)

Instructions regarding War Diaries and Intelligence Summaries are contained in F. S. Regs., Part II. and the Staff Manual respectively. Title pages will be prepared in manuscript.

Place	Date	Hour	Summary of Events and Information	Remarks and references to Appendices
In the trenches	March 1917			
	1st		The enemy fires about 9 Minenwerfer during the day & evening on DURHAM ROAD.; X 36 retaliated with SA, effectually silencing him. From the Battn report the 18th V 36 carried on work on their position at DURHAM ROAD & also at ANTON'S FARM	
	4th		X 36 were relieved in the line by Y 36. V Bty's GOOSEBERRY FARM position was altered to fire further north in preparation for expected heavy	
	5th		At 9 a.m. the bosche fires 3 medium T.M.s on T 6 5 & Y 36 retaliates with 6 rounds on N 36 B 5.6.	
	6th		Three medium Minenwerfer fell in DAY STREET about N 36 C 6.0 to which Y 36 retaliated with 2 rounds on N 36 B 5.6 & 6 on N 36 D 2.6. About 3 p.m. the enemy sent over 6 medium "Minnies" to which Y Bty replied with 9 rounds on N 36 B 2.6 & 1. 1 rounds on T 6 B 8.9 roaming silence on Stand-to.	
	7th		During the afternoon, from 1.30 to 3.5 p.m., medium & light T.M.s were fired into the bosche in V Bty's sector; J & 14 Trench Mortars 5.A5	
	8th		A heavy Minenwerfer was active between N 36 & T 6 & a few Pineapples with 25 rounds by Y Bty, who also dispersed 34 during a storage shower.	

WAR DIARY
or
INTELLIGENCE SUMMARY

Army Form C. 2118.

Place	Date	Hour	Summary of Events and Information	Remarks and references to Appendices
In trenches	March 1917 8th		by the Huns at 3.30. One of the gun pits suffered from a direct hit after Y. Department has met with severe damage in conjunction with heavy artillery. V Bty fires 150 rounds on Engr-outs at V.2.C.90.45.	
	11th		X Bty relieves at ANTON'S FARM Z Bty who commences training at NEUVE EGLISE on the following day.	
	17th		Y 36 took over from X 16 in R.E. FARM Sector & J 36 took over positions from Z 16.	
	18th		The Anzacs took over from X 36 at ANTON'S FARM & X Bty relieves Y Bty at R.E. FARM. V Bty handed over to New Zealanders & took over new sector from 18th Division.	
	19th		About 10 air-scouts were fired by the enemy on DEAD MAN'S FARM & X 36 replies with HH fuzes. J Bty fires 10 rounds on N.30.A.72.16 in retaliation to machine gun harassing fire.	
	20th		In reply to a few oil-cans on KINGSWAY X Bty expends 30 rounds (V flat) 5 rounds were fired on N.30.C.08.69 in retaliation by J Bty.	
	21st		X 36 fires 36 rounds in retaliation to a few minenwerfer, & J Bty out	

WAR DIARY or INTELLIGENCE SUMMARY.

(Erase heading not required.)

Army Form C. 2118.

Place	Date	Hour	Summary of Events and Information	Remarks and references to Appendices
In the trenches	March 19	21st Contd	were with 30 rounds. V Bty also held a house-shafts position.	
	22nd		In retaliation X Bty expended 8 4 3" Bty, 6 2" bombs.	
	24th		The enemy shelled S.P. Post heavily in H a.m.) Scoring direct hits on two of X Bty's emplacements partially blew trench in retaliation to enemy minning of heavy T.M. guns were expended by Z36	
	25th		Y Bty relieves X Bty in the line & fires 2 rounds from N 30 C 57.2. V Bty relieves W of R.E. FARM position so S.L. to enable a 70° arc to be obtained. This work having been commenced on the 19th inst. 3 Bty fires 50 rounds on enemy wire.	
	26th		Successful wire cutting was carried out by J 36.	
	28th		Y Bty fires 15 rounds on wire at N 30 C 10.75 & also knocks no pieces of a concrete enemy dug-out.	
	29th		30thly five rounds were fired on wire at N 30 C 05.90 by Y Bty who also retaliates to H. Heavy Minenwerfer with 6 bombs on N 30 C 32.00	
	30th		Y Bty discharges 30 rounds on wire at N 29 R 80.00 & retaliates with 5 rounds on N 30 C 35.85 to 2 heavy Minenwerfer shots fired about N 29 R 80.00	

WAR DIARY
or
INTELLIGENCE SUMMARY.

Army Form C. 2118.

Place	Date	Hour	Summary of Events and Information	Remarks and references to Appendices
Authuille	March 1917	30th Contd	Z Bty bombarded the Boche front line – N 30 b 10.95 to N 30 b 20.55 with 61 rounds, besides firing 40 "punishment" 12 rounds on N 30 A 10.00 & "1 rounds on N 30 C 10.90.	4
		3 pm	At 12 noon Y Bty registered with 10 rounds on N 36 A 6.5.	

N.K.Smith
Capt, R.H.A.
T.M.S.O. 36th Div Arty.

Army Form C. 2118.

36th Dvl Trench Mortar Batteries

WAR DIARY
INTELLIGENCE SUMMARY.
(Erase heading not required.)

Instructions regarding War Diaries and Intelligence Summaries are contained in F. S. Regs., Part II. and the Staff Manual respectively. Title pages will be prepared in manuscript.

Place	Date	Hour	Summary of Events and Information	Remarks and references to Appendices
In the trenches	April 1st		A temporary position was constructed by Z 36 Bty at N 30 A 00.80 for use sitting on NAPLES TRENCH	
	3rd		X 36 Bty completed a bomb store commenced at R.E. FARM previous day & started work on defensive positions	
	4th		Work on defence positions was completed by X Bty who fired 60 bombs on enemy front line with good effect	
	5th		It was noticed that enemy retaliation was very weak as BULLY BEEF FARM & Avenues to trenches two two front line was very fly lost.	
	6th		Sorty. there bombs were fires on enemy front line by X Bty	
	9th		Z Bty constructed a temporary position at N 29 B 91.20 to cover left half of NARROW TRENCH	
	10th		Enemy trench mortar fires at were at N.30 C 15.55 by X Bty, but the wind was too strong for good shooting.	
	12th		X Bty fires 36 trench mortar bombs were at N 30 C 25.55 making a gap from 25 to 30 yds wide. This Bty also fires 24 trench m retaliation for enemy Minenwerfer.	

WAR DIARY of INTELLIGENCE SUMMARY.

(Erase heading not required.)

Army Form C. 2118.

Place	Date	Hour	Summary of Events and Information	Remarks and references to Appendices
In the trenches	Apl '13		X Bty fires 32 rounds at enemy wire at N 30 C 12.56, making 10 x gaps. Enemy rounds were also fired in retaliation for enemy "burries" which fell in his own line. A temporary position was made at N 29 B 79.05 to cover left of SPANBROEK re-entrant & NARROW LANE. The Bosche retaliation to our fire continues to be weak.	4.Z./Bty
	16th		X Bty fires 40 rounds at N 30 ST (14 with the Temple Silencer) on enemy & front line. The short pony movement.	
	18th		From PICCADILLY X Bty fires S 31 rounds on enemy wire. 30 rounds in retaliation.	
	22nd to 26th		440 rounds were expended by X Bty in cutting wire, harassing & transfer of retaliation.	
	20th		Between 3.30 & 4 pm. V 36 Heavy T.M. Bty fires 114 rounds at N 30 C 96.05 on a front where enemy seems to have crossed rounds of the 114 rounds dropped short. Falling 250 yards in front of the A.T.L. All others burst well.	
	23rd		The T.M. Batteries were shelled one of rear billets at DONEGAL FARM.	

Army Form C. 2118.

WAR DIARY
—or—
INTELLIGENCE SUMMARY.
(Erase heading not required.)

Instructions regarding War Diaries and Intelligence Summaries are contained in F.S. Regs., Part II. and the Staff Manual respectively. Title pages will be prepared in manuscript.

Place	Date	Hour	Summary of Events and Information	Remarks and references to Appendices
In the Dunes	23rd Contd.		Three men being wounded.	
	24th		The enemy appeared to press his front line more strongly on fire more than formerly & resorted to severe outbursts of 77 m.m. shells. He also retaliated with Granatenwerfer from his support line. V 36 Heavy T.M. Bty fired 20 rounds between 4 & 4.35 p.m.	
	26th		being the same as for the shoot on the 20th.	
	29th		A temporary lull was placed by Z Bty at N 29 D 17.9 9.4 in order to assist fire front from the same position.	
	30th		The Boche retaliated rightfully to fire by Z. Bty at 6.30 p.m. with Granatenwerfer bombs. He appears to have three T.M.'s always ready for immediate action. He needs a total rate of fire. Y 36 Bty was employed throughout the month in harassing 2nd T.M.	
	Total.		positions along the whole of the Divisional front.	

A.T. Hudson Capt RFA
D.T.M.O. 36th Division

2353 Wt. W2544/1454 700,000 5/15 D. D. & L. A.D.S.S./Forms/C. 2118.

Army Form C. 2118.

36th Divl Artillery Trench Mortar Batteries

WAR DIARY
or
INTELLIGENCE SUMMARY.
(Erase heading not required.)

Place	Date	Hour	Summary of Events and Information	Remarks and references to Appendices
In the field	May 1st		X 36 Bty fired 100 rounds from two guns on left of KINGSWAY in support of a daylight raid & Z 36 Bty expended 150 rounds, the result in each case being very satisfactory. V 36 Bty were engaged in constructing three heavy T.M. positions	
	2nd		Forty rounds were fired by X Bty from KINGSWAY in retaliation to enemy fire, while Z Bty sent over 70 rounds to enemy front line from N 30 A 33.19 to N 30 A 28.07 provoking only slight retaliation. Short shoots were carried out by both X & Z Batteries which expended 30 & 70 rounds respectively, the objective being the enemy wire. The results seemed to show that this type of shooting can be carried out with success.	
	4th			
	5th		X Bty were engaged in cutting wire, effectively discharging 25 bombs. Dug-outs & front line in SPANBROEKMOLEN were bombarded with 90 rounds by Z Bty	
	6th			
	7th		Wire cutting was carried out by X Bty. With 85 bombs Z Bty also cut wire in preparation for a dummy raid on the following day.	

WAR DIARY
or
INTELLIGENCE SUMMARY

Army Form C. 2118.

Place	Date	Hour	Summary of Events and Information	Remarks and references to Appendices
In the trees	May 8th		Firing 40 rounds, Z Bty took part in strong raids, laying two mortars on enemy's front & support lines. The shooting was effective, as was also that of X Bty who expended 20 rounds for the purpose of destruction. V Bty commenced digging another position & X Bty sent over 10 bombs in retaliation.	
	9th		Enemy mortars were very active in the DURHAM ROAD Sector, X Bty firing 28 rounds in retaliation.	
	10th		Working parties were heard in crater at N 30 A 53.58 & on this target Z Bty sent over 100 rounds. From PICCADILLY X Bty utilised 34 bombs in cutting wire.	
	11th		The bns at the position started by V Bty on the 9th was completed. Both X & Z Batteries were engaged in wire cutting, their shoots being effectively carried out. The delivery of M.O. ammunition commenced.	
	12th			
	13th		X Bty expended 30 rounds on enemy's wire & Z Bty 20 rounds on earthworks at N 30 A 53.58.	
	14th			
	15th		Shooting was confined to enemy's wire, X & Z Batteries doing much damage	

WAR DIARY or INTELLIGENCE SUMMARY

Army Form C. 2118

Place	Date	Hour	Summary of Events and Information	Remarks and references to Appendices
In the trees	May 18th	Contd	with 44 & 45 rounds respectively.	
	19th 20th		Two heavy T.M. positions were dug by parties of the Divisional Infantry. From this date until the 24th. X & Z Batteries took part in wire-cutting operations. The shooting was very effective, over 1300 rounds being expended. Both X & Z Batteries were relieved by the 32nd Divisional T.M's & on the 29th. V Bty mounts a gun & handed this, together with 469 heavy rounds, over to V 32 T.M. Bty.	
	28th		During the month Y 36 Bty was solely engaged in working upon the various positions in the Divisional sector & it's done very good work. Y 36 Heavy Battery also worked day & night on the gun emplacements, bomb stores, dug-outs etc., undertaken &, besides large quantities of building material, the Batteries carried over 6000 rounds of 2-inch & over 900 rounds of 9.45-inch M.O. ammunition.	
	Note :-			

H. Armstrong
Capt. R.F.A.
D.T.M.O. 36 Division

D.T.M.O.
36TH
DIVL. ARTILLERY.
No. 1
Date 31. 5. 19

Army Form C. 2118.

WAR DIARY
INTELLIGENCE SUMMARY. 36th Div. T.M. Batteries.
(Erase heading not required.)

Vol 12

Instructions regarding War Diaries and Intelligence Summaries are contained in F.S. Regs., Part II. and the Staff Manual respectively. Title pages will be prepared in manuscript.

Place	Date	Hour	Summary of Events and Information	Remarks and references to Appendices
In the Field	June 1917 1.		V Battery registers three heavy mortars & fires 100 rounds on mine shaft at N 30 C.6.0, BONE POINT, & enemy's reserve line at N 30 B.02.08.	
	2.		V Bty engaged the same targets as on the previous day, expending 164 rounds.	
	3.		X 36 relieves X 32, Y 36 relieves Y 32, & Z 36 relieves Z 32 T.M. Batteries in the line. V Bty fires 108 rounds at same points as on two preceding days.	
	4.		Wire-cutting operations were commenced by all the 2-inch Batteries, X Bty expending 70, Y Bty 109 & Z Bty 353 bombs. V Bty got a long-range heavy mortar in position & registers with five rounds on L'ENFER WOOD	
	5.		Over one thousand rounds were fired by X, Y, & Z Batteries in cutting wire, whilst 92 heavy bombs were dropped in L'ENFER WOOD by V Battery.	
	6.		The 2-inch Batteries carried out another wire-cutting shoot, after which X & Z 36, together with the heavy Battery, returned to rest camp near SHELTER FARM. Two heavy German shells completely demolishes the	

WAR DIARY
INTELLIGENCE SUMMARY
(Erase heading not required.)

Army Form C. 2118.

Place	Date	Hour	Summary of Events and Information	Remarks and references to Appendices
Jues	June 6.—Contd		fire in the afternoon. This was "Zero Day." X Bty helps A/143 R.F.A to get into action in forward position near REGENT STREET dug-outs. Y Bty assists C/143 R.F.A to get into action after advance of the Infantry, afterwards returning to SHELTER FARM billets. Z Bty assists D/143 R.F.A to get into action in forward position near REGENT STREET Dug-outs & V36.	
	7.		X Bty helps B/143 R.F.A into forward Battery position. X Bty finds a German "oil-can" gun in the enemy's OS support line & Z Bty recovers from the same a light Minenwerfer & 138 rounds of ammunition. Both guns & bombs being brought back to billets. The Medium Batteries brought all their mortars & equipment out of the line.	
	8.			
	9.			
	10.		X & Z Batteries sent eight men to II ANZAC Corps at HOUPLINES & Y Bty eight men to II ANZAC Corps at STEENWERCK.	
	11.		An officer & six men of V Bty were sent to fire a long-range 9.45-inch T.M. for the ANZACS. The detachments sent to the ANZAC	

WAR DIARY
INTELLIGENCE SUMMARY.
(Erase heading not required.)

Army Form C. 2118.

Place	Date	Hour	Summary of Events and Information	Remarks and references to Appendices
Jules	June 11th	Cont.	Corps from X, Y, & Z Batteries returned to billets.	
	15.		The Medium Batteries moved from SHELTER FARM to a field near ST JANS CAPPEL.	
	16.		Systematic training was commenced by Medium Batteries who were joined in Camp by V Heavy Battery.	
	24.		All Batteries removed to DRANOUTRE where training was continued & working parties provided for the Divisional Ammunition Column.	

N.Y. Gibson
Capt R.F.A.
D.T.M.O. 36th Division

D.T.M.O.
36TH
DIVL. ARTILLERY.
No.
B.Pie. 6.17

Army Form C. 2118.

D.T.M.O.
WAR DIARY DIVL. ARTILLERY.
or INTELLIGENCE SUMMARY
(Erase heading not required.)

36th Divisional T.M. Batteries

Place	Date	Hour	Summary of Events and Information	Remarks and references to Appendices
Fields.	July 1-5		X36, Y36, Z36 & V36 T.M. Batteries furnishes the 36th Divl. Amm. Column with fatigue parties for the purpose of collecting ammunition from Battery positions after the WYTSCHAETE-MESSINES advance.	
	6		All Batteries marches off from DRANOUTRE to hut Camp near POPERINGHE Sheet 28 N.W. G10C1.6.2.	
	7		The Medium Battery Commander, accompanied by the T.M. Officers of the 55th Division, visits the batteries in front of ST. JEAN & reconnoitres positions for M.O.	
	8-19		Each of the three Medium Batteries was engaged in constructing three positions, & V/36 Bty two heavy positions in the ST.JEAN - WIELTJE front. Light parties carries 2-inch, 6-inch & 9.45" inch ammunition to the various positions.	
	20		V/36 & Z/36 Batteries each fires 150 rounds of 2" ammunition in enemy's wire.	
	21		V/36. fires 25 rounds from long range mortar & 10 rounds from short range mortar on CAMBRAI SUPPORT. The Medium Batteries	

Army Form C. 2118.

WAR DIARY
of L. ARTILLERY
D.T.M.O.

INTELLIGENCE SUMMARY
(Erase heading not required.)

Instructions regarding War Diaries and Intelligence Summaries are contained in F.S. Regs., Part II. and the Staff Manual respectively. Title Pages will be prepared in manuscript.

Place	Date July	Hour	Summary of Events and Information	Remarks and references to Appendices
Sués	21 Cents.		were engaged in wire-cutting, which they did with success, the following rounds being expended: X.36 214, Y.36 200, Z.36 120.	
	22		Wire-cutting was continued X, Y & Z Batteries firing 161, 150 & 50 rounds respectively. A premature burst with No 1 gun of X.36 Bty resulted in No 45349 Cpl R.J. Condons being killed & No 26366 Gr R.W. Rees being wounded.	
	23		Sifty heavy trench mortars were fired on CAMBRAI SUPPORT by V Battery, 10 with long range mortars & his will short range mortar. X, Y & Z Batteries again cut the enemys wire with 130, 102 & 120 rounds respectively.	
	26.		With the short range T.M. V/36 Bty sent over 25 rounds to CAMBRAI SUPPORT. X Bty fires 330 rounds from 6 inch Stokes mortar & Z Bty 50 rounds of 2-inch & 60 rounds of 6-inch on enemys wire & CALL TRENCH.	
	27.		Y Bty took a party of 50 men from the 36th D.A.G. up the line & carried 6-inch & 2-inch ammunition to the positions, besides firing 96 rounds on the Boche wire.	

2449 Wt. W14957/M90 750,000 1/16 J.B.C. & A. Forms/C.2118/12.

WAR DIARY or INTELLIGENCE SUMMARY

Army Form C. 2118.

Place	Date	Hour	Summary of Events and Information	Remarks and references to Appendices
Ieds.	July 28		X/36 fires 11 rounds from short range battery on CAMBRAI SUPPORT, & fly effectively expends 70 rounds of 6-inch Stokes ammunition.	
	29.		Z/36 fires 60 rounds of 6-inch ammunition on enemy trench line. W/36 CALI SUPPORT & 1142 rounds of 6-inch ammo on front line were CALIFORNIA & CALI TRENCH.	
	30.		All batteries out of action. Sixty men were supplied to the R.A.C. to assist in work with ammunition.	
	31.		Three officers & 36 men proceeded to help forward batteries into action & bring up their spare ammunition.	

L.K. Trenton Capt. R.F.A.
D.T.M.O. 36 Division.

Army Form C. 2118.

WAR DIARY
or
INTELLIGENCE SUMMARY

(Erase heading not required.)

36th Divisional Trench Mortars

Place	Date	Hour	Summary of Events and Information	Remarks and references to Appendices
Ques	August 14			
	1-12		All Batteries were awaiting the 36th Divisional Ammunition Column at STANLEY DUMP near VLAMERTINGHE.	
	3		V/36 T.M. Battery took over two 9.45" TMs from the 55th Divl Artillery.	
	11		X/36 Battery started carrying 6-inch newton mortars & ammunition to CAPRICORN TRENCH in front of WIELTJE.	
	13		X/36 Battery built positions for 6-inch Mortars & carries up the remainder of ammunition. Detachments from Y, Z, & V/36 Batteries were attached to these Batteries to lend assistance in connection with the operations in progress.	
	14		X Battery completes 6" positions & fires 86 rounds on wire at POND FARM, afterwards returning to rest billets.	
	16		Two gunners of Y Battery were wounded while working with an 18-pr Battery; one of the gunners eventually succumbs to his wounds &c.	

Army Form C. 2118.

D.T.M.O.
36TH
DIVL. ARTILLERY.

36th Divisional Trench Mortars

WAR DIARY or INTELLIGENCE SUMMARY

(Erase heading not required.)

Place	Date	Hour	Summary of Events and Information	Remarks and references to Appendices
Suets	August '14 19		2nd Lieut D.P. DICKSON was invalided to England, his foot crushed by a railway truck whilst superintending operations at STANLEY DUMP on the 14th.	
	21.		Three Canadiens were suffered by detachment of 2 V/36 Battery supporting a Seels Battery. One gunner was killed & one Corporal & one gunner were wounded. This Battery ranges are for 9.45" T.M's to the 61st Divisional Artillery.	
	22.		2/Lieut R.N. STRANGER, V/36 Battery, was wounded whilst serving with 2/173rd Bde R.F.A.	
	23.		Lieut J. CUTHBERT, Z/36 Battery, was attached temporarily to command V Battery.	
	24.		All Batteries were conveyed in motor lorries from Camp near POPERINGHE to the WINNEZEELE Artillery Rest Area.	
	26.		The C.R.A., 36th Division, inspected all Batteries at rest Camp.	

Army Form C. 2118.

WAR DIARY
or
INTELLIGENCE SUMMARY

(Erase heading not required.)

36th Divisional Trench Mortars

Place	Date August 17	Hour	Summary of Events and Information	Remarks and references to Appendices
Dees	29.		X/36 Battery entrained at CASSEL & Y, Z & V/36 Batteries at ESQUELBECQ for BAPAUME. From the latter names place the Batteries were conveyed by light Railway to ROCQUIGNY, thence marching to "K" Camp near LE MESNIL EN ARROUAISE	
	31.		In the morning the G.O.C., 36th Division inspected the Batteries at "K" Camp & later in the day Detachments proceeded to HAVRINCOURT WOOD & took over Dug-outs from the 9th Division	

French Mortars

M. Henson
Captain R.F.A.
D.T.M.O. 36th Division

[Stamp: D.T.M.O. 36TH DIVL. ARTILLERY. No. ___ Date. 3.9.17]

Army Form C. 2118.

36th Divisional Trench M/lays

Vol 15

WAR DIARY
or
INTELLIGENCE SUMMARY
(Erase heading not required.)

Instructions regarding War Diaries and Intelligence Summaries are contained in F.S. Regs., Part II. and the Staff Manual respectively. Title Pages will be prepared in manuscript.

Place	Date	Hour	Summary of Events and Information	Remarks and references to Appendices
Dues	Sept 1914 1st		All Batteries took over positions from the 9th Division.	
	2nd		Y/36 Battery registers hostile on zero lines between 4pm & 9pm from 2.30 till dawn stood to at request of Infantry C.O. in case the enemy attempted to retake advanced airposts recently captured by us. V Battery fires three rounds from Yorkshire Bank (K32 A&B), with Dean Copse (K32 b 85.40) & Elna Copses (K26 d 90.25) as targets.	
	3		V Battery again fires from Yorkshire Bank & X Battery selected positions in the Hermies sector.	
	5.		2nd Lieut (A/Capt) R.R. Sharp, M.C., took over command of Y/36 Heavy Battery. X Battery fires two rounds in retaliation on K26 b 6.30 & fires rounds on K26 b 43.10.	

WAR DIARY or INTELLIGENCE SUMMARY

Army Form C. 2118.

Place	Date	Hour	Summary of Events and Information	Remarks and references to Appendices
Trees	Sept 7th 1917		With the object of silencing a light Minenwerfer, V Battery fires 4 rounds from the Yorkshire Bank position & were apparently successful. Two rounds were fires by X Battery at working party at K.26.d.02.9. At least one man was hit, as loud screams followed. Lewis screams report as follows.	
	8th		X Battery fires 6 rounds & 6 rounds on K.26.b.10.20. Y Bty fires 4 rounds on K.26.d.20.93 & 6 rounds in retaliation for two medium Minenwerfer which fell on K.32.d.	
	9th		In retaliation X Battery fires 4 rounds on K.26.b.15.25.	
	10th		One long-range 9.45" T.M. was reaches from Ordnance by V Battery.	
	11th		V Battery fires 4 rounds of one long bomb from short range mortar at Yorkshire Bank & one long bomb in retaliation. To eight medium	

WAR DIARY or INTELLIGENCE SUMMARY

Army Form C. 2118.

Place	Date	Hour	Summary of Events and Information	Remarks and references to Appendices
Jues	Sept 11th 1917		Minenwerfer which fell on our outpost line Y Bty retaliated with 15 rounds on Etna B (K26d 90.25). At 10.15 p.m. Y Bty fires 15 rounds on Etna in accordance with nightfiring programme.	
	12th		V Battery fires three rounds from Yorkshire Bank Long-range mortar. Y Battery registers on Etna (K26d 90.25) with four rounds in night firing operation. X Bty fires 20 rounds on Canal Coppse (K32 c 65.90) & Y Battery 20 rounds on Dean Coppse (K32 c 65.90)	
	13th		V Battery fires 5 rounds on Showden (K27d 35.20) & 5 rounds on Boggart's Hole (K33 b 1.4) in accordance with nightly during programme. Ten rounds were fired from the Yorkshire Bank Long range heavy with Verviers (K27 c 20.60) as target. Y Bty fires 3 rounds on Dean Coppse (K32 b 85.40) in registration, afterwards shooting on the Canal of feature with 40 rounds & engaging Etna (K26d 90.25) also with 40 rounds.	

WAR DIARY or INTELLIGENCE SUMMARY

Army Form C. 2118.

Place	Date	Hour	Summary of Events and Information	Remarks and references to Appendices
Fields	13th Jan Contd		Y Battery also engaged 14 rounds in retaliation for heavy T.M. which fell on Yorkshire Bank (K26d.90.25)	
	14th		(K26d.90.25) for the same purpose. Twenty-four rounds were fired by V Bty on Roggart's Hole (K33.b.1.4) & a few rounds at K.24.c.6.6. in retaliation 4 heavy rounds were fired on K.27.c.20.75 & H 2-inch trench mortar were fired by X Bty in retaliation on K 26 b 15.25	
	15th		Vesuvius (K.27.c.20.60) was engaged by V Bty with 4 rounds & 5 heavy bombs were fired on K 26 c in accordance with night-firing programme.	
	16th		A hostile T.M. at K.21.c.10.10 was fired on by V Bty (4 rounds) & X Bty carried out an operation order by Bty of firing 5 rounds by discharging 5" rounds on K 26 d 40.40.	
	17th		X Bty fired 3 rounds on Canal Copse (K26.b.15.40) & 5 rounds on Organ Copse (K26.d.2.4) & Infantry Bty of fired 5 rounds with Bean Copse (K33.b.85.40) as objective	

Army Form C. 2118.

WAR DIARY or INTELLIGENCE SUMMARY

(Erase heading not required.)

Place	Date	Hour.	Summary of Events and Information	Remarks and references to Appendices
Sees	Sept 18th		Five rounds were fired on rear trench in K.26.b by V Bty in retaliation. This Battery also fires 2 rounds on Vermeries (K.27c.20.60) in accordance with night-firing programme. X Bty at 9.21p.m. two rounds on K.26.b.2.8. & in a period of a premature no A.6.31c. Capt P.G. Eastaus, R.G.A. (V Bty) was wounded in the Face & a Temple licence damaged.	
	19th		Two towers were observed on Vermeries (K.27c.20.60) by V Bty & V Bty fires 6 rounds on Pive (K.26.A.70.25), provoking no retaliation.	
	20th		X Battery fired 10 set rounds on Vermeries (K.27c.20.60). V Bty fires 15 rounds on defences target from K.26.b.4.0 to K.26.b.5.3. Z Bty, with two howitzer supports 50 rounds on trench from K.26.b.4.0 to K.26.b.5.3.	
	21st		A Gunner of V/Bty was wounded in the Shoulder by a Piece of shell from an explosion of a Gun in a Bty farther on our right and a British aircraft	

WAR DIARY or INTELLIGENCE SUMMARY

Army Form C. 2118.

VI

Place	Date	Hour	Summary of Events and Information	Remarks and references to Appendices
Trees	1917 Sept 21		During programme X Bty fired 34 rounds on trench from K.26.d.10.45 to K.26.d.50.90.	
	22.		Y Bty registers with 20 rounds on wire at K.26.d.20.35.	
	25.		Between 1.15 p.m. & 3 p.m. enemy fired about 30 rounds on K.32.b.0.6 - K.32.A.6.4. & fired up a patrol of Y/36 Bty at K.35 around in a trench line. Y Bty returns hostile from this point & fires 5 rounds in registration on K.32.b.6.4. In accordance with heat destruction programme Y Bty fires 11 rounds at extensive target from K.26.d.38.60 to K.26.d.40.60 as well as 10 rounds into the village of HAVRINCOURT. A bombardment of the wire between K.26.d.6.4. & K.26.d.20.35 was carried out by Y Bty who expended 143 rounds; the enemy retaliated with 12 heavy TMs on K.32.d.55.65 & 3 rounds ... on K.32.A.4.4.	
	26.		A working party south of (Organ Copse (K.26.d.2.4.) was fired at by Y Bty, two rounds of (silence) being used.	

WAR DIARY or INTELLIGENCE SUMMARY

Army Form C. 2118.

VII

Place	Date	Hour	Summary of Events and Information	Remarks and references to Appendices
Sucs	1914 Sept 28th		Three rounds in retaliation were fired on Boggart Hole (K33f1.4) by V Bty & Elsa (K36d 90.25) received 10 rounds from Y Bty in accordance with Night operations programme.	
	29.		Y Bty carried out night-firing on Wigan Copse (K36d 2.4) & X Bty engaged Canal Copse (K26b 15.40) with 10 rounds.	
	30.		Registering Programme X Bty first 10 rounds at K26b 5.9 L = K26d 5.9.	

A.H.Hinton, Captain R.G.A.
D.T.M.O., 36th Division

D.T.M.O.,
36TH
DIVL. ARTILLERY.
No.
Date 1.10.14.

Army Form C. 2118.

WAR DIARY
or
INTELLIGENCE SUMMARY.

36th Divisional Trench Mortar Batteries

Vol 16

(Erase heading not required.)

Instructions regarding War Diaries and Intelligence Summaries are contained in F.S. Regs., Part II. and the Staff Manual respectively. Title pages will be prepared in manuscript.

Place	Date	Hour	Summary of Events and Information	Remarks and references to Appendices
Field	1917 Feb 2		V Battery fires 6. rounds from short range gun at Q.3.f.35.30 for detonator purposes on BOGGARTS HOLE, K.33.b. At 11 a.m. V Bty fires 10 rounds on wire at K.26.d.45.25 with good effect. At 9 p.m. fires amm. rounds into ETNA, K.26.d.	
	3		At 3.15 a.m. Y Bty fires two rounds into ETNA, K.26.d., previous to a fighting patrol going out. On returning the patrol reported movement in ETNA. Y Bty engages these more rounds on this target. At 11.30 a.m. Y Bty registered a gun in a temporary position on wire at K.26.a.40.25 with 55 rounds; at 3.30 p.m. they are were at this point with 42 rounds, two guns being in action.	
	4.		V Battery fires 24 heavy bombs from gun at YORKSHIRE BANK, K.32.a & b., with good effect.	

WAR DIARY or INTELLIGENCE SUMMARY

Army Form C. 2118.

Place	Date Oct 1917	Hour	Summary of Events and Information	Remarks and references to Appendices
Fees	5.		Hostile artillery was active in the junction of YORKSHIRE BANK, K3b & d. At 6 a.m. Y Battery fired 4 rounds on ETNA, K26d, where four of the enemy were seen to enter. From 9 a.m. to 11.30 a.m. 60 5.9's fell along the valley of YORKSHIRE BANK, K3b & d.	
	6.		Expending 54 rounds, X Bty. carried out wire cutting at K26d 10.36. Y Battery processes on Cuttings to the 12th Divisional area.	
	7.		Y Battery joined the 12th Division at ARRAS, travelling via DOULLENS & spending the night at PREVENT. On the regiment of the infantry X Bty fires 4 rounds on ETNA, K26d, to score a TMB.	
	8.		Y Battery went into the Line with the 13th Bde THF on front of MONCHY-LE-PREUX. Eleven rounds of 6" ammunition were fires by Z Bty on SPOIL HEAP, K20 & c. via Light Minenwerfer. The enemy retaliating with a M/M c.w. gun.	

WAR DIARY
or
INTELLIGENCE SUMMARY

Army Form C. 2118.

Place	Date 1917 Oct.	Hour	Summary of Events and Information	Remarks and references to Appendices
Trees	10.		Z Bty fires 60 2" (ombs from two guns in R.3 on enemy wire & 66 rounds of 6" ammunition on wire on the north side of SPOIL HEAP K.20.a.0.c. The enemy retaliated heavily on our MEBU.Schreiner emplacement.	
	11.		Thirty rounds from 6" mortar were fired by Z Battery on K.20.a.6.4.4. to silence a Light Minenwerfer which was active at night. This Battery sent one five rounds of 2 inch ammunition.	
	13.		X Battery expended 20 6" bombs in registration in accordance with 13th Div Arty operation order Y Bty bombarded the enemy's trenches for ex hours in face of heavy retaliation. Enemy aeroplanes were very active and our positions apparently for the purpose of observation & directing fire on our positions, apparently. Y Bty left MONCHY to report to 3rd Artillery positions.	
	15.		Z Bty expenses 55 rounds from 6" mortar on enemy's wire at SPOIL HEAP	

WAR DIARY or INTELLIGENCE SUMMARY

Army Form C. 2118.

Place	Date 1917	Hour	Summary of Events and Information	Remarks and references to Appendices
Ypres	Oct 15	Cont.	K20a & c. V Bty fires 5 rounds on K21a 5.4, 10 rounds on K21c 10.0.2 & 6 rounds on K21c 43.04 in accordance with Corps Programme. The enemy retaliates with 10 rounds from a 10.5 cm How. for the purpose of registration. X Bty fires ten 6" rounds on K33 c 48.83.	
	17		X Bty fires 30 6" rounds on enemy Minenwerfer, which fell at 3.15 pm on K13 a 6.3. Y Bty retaliates with 6 rounds on WIGAN, K26d. Z Battery fires 34 2" rounds on enemy wire at K26a 3.8 d 34 6" rounds on were at K20a 9.5.	
	18		The C.R.A., 36th Division, wittresses the works stores in the line by V Bty on SNOWDON, K27d, in retaliation to 50 rounds of German Gunfire YORKSHIRE BANK Minenwerfer on our front line. One heavy mortar at BUTLER'S CROSS	
	19			
	20		V Battery fires two rounds from Long Tom's Gun at	Q36

WAR DIARY or INTELLIGENCE SUMMARY

Army Form C. 2118.

Place	Date	Hour	Summary of Events and Information	Remarks and references to Appendices
Trees	20th Dec 1917 Contd		fires to towards our BOGGART'S HOLE, K.33.b, for registration. The shoots being very successful. The enemy replied with 10 rounds from a 10.5cm gun on our trenches near TRESCAULT & 3 heavy Minnenwerfer on YORKSHIRE VALLEY, while 4 heavy Minnenwerfer were fired, with our positions at K.32.a.25.40 as target.	
	21.		At about 5.30 p.m. the enemy heavy trench mortars opened on one of V Bty's mortars with a heavy Minnenwerfer. At 6.15 p.m. V Bty fired 4th round on wire west of WIGAN, K.26.d & Cuilbien Gap. The enemy retaliated with four heavy Minnenwerfer on K.31.a.30.44. One of V Bty's Lng. range guns at YORKSHIRE BANK fired 4 rounds on VESUVIUS, K.24.c. in retaliation to 4 heavy Minnenwerfer. Another round from V Bty's gun at BUTLER'S CROSS Q.36., were fired on K.34.c.3.3. between 12 noon & 1 p.m.; Touching a hit Direct hits on Capt McBrien's Minenwerfer has been active during the morning firing 30 Minenwerfer from trenches between SYKE ALLEY & BUTLER'S CROSS. Z Bty covered our trenches were with 50 rounds from 2 inch T.M's.	5
	22.		The enemy's	

WAR DIARY or INTELLIGENCE SUMMARY

Army Form C. 2118.

Place	Date	Hour	Summary of Events and Information	Remarks and references to Appendices
Trees	1914 Dec 24.		V Bty at 3.15 pm. fired 6 rounds from long-range gun at YORKSHIRE BANK & at 2.15 pm 12 rounds from gun at BUTLER'S CROSS. BOGGART'S HOLE as target. Between 2 pm & 2.30 pm the enemy fired 6 rounds of [shrapnel?] T.N.T. our positions at BUTLER'S CROSS evidently being the target. The trials were dispersed on BOGGART'S HOLE, K 33 b, by X Bty, whilst Z Battery ranges & stores & were between K 20 c 92.52 & K 20 c 65.55 – 55.63	6
	25.		X Bty fires 26 rounds on come from K 33 d 14.44 & L K 33 d 13 mm. Whilst firing at home at K 33 d 15.43 one round fell short at K 33 d 15.43 in full view of the enemy who were in a trench. Guns were appeared to have been fired. Cpl 2 f Y Bty commence to shoot at the later near WIGAN & enter two small gaps. The twentieth rounds fell abnormally short & killed No 91146 Br C Whithouse R.F.A. The gun pit was badly damaged by early bombardments.	

WAR DIARY or INTELLIGENCE SUMMARY

Army Form C. 2118.

Place	Date	Hour	Summary of Events and Information	Remarks and references to Appendices
Suez	Oct 25th 1914	cont²	but the remainder of the detachment were unhurt. Whilst firing from a 2 inch emplacement in K.19.d., to frustrate an enemy with Z Bty, killing No 39909 Corpl A.G. Newman, R.G.A., almost instantly. Concerning the late Corpl Newman the O/C, Z/56 T.M.Bty wrote: This unfortunate N.C.O. whilst attending to the safety of his detachment has suffered the penalty of so doing. As a lover of Home Life. His high character as a soldier & his genial nature endeared him to his comrades & his unfortunate loss came as a great shock to the Officers, N.C.O's & men of the battery."	
	26.		From New Russian Lines at YORKSHIRE BANK K.19.c. two rounds on VESUVIUS, K.29.c. At the request of the Infantry Y/Bty provides covering fire for to hrs patrol which went out to WIGAN at 6.55 p.m., dispersing 15 enemy. Z battery fires 13.6" hostile on enemy wire in front of SPOIL HEAP, K.20.a.&.c.	

WAR DIARY or INTELLIGENCE SUMMARY

Army Form C. 2118.

Place: Trees

Date 1914 Oct	Hour	Summary of Events and Information	Remarks
27		At 2.30 p.m. the enemy fires on YORKSHIRE BANK with Light Howitzer. Y Bty retaliates with 5 rounds on K26d 50 y's where shell stopped. At 4.30 a.m. medium TM's with "fish tails" fell across YORKSHIRE BANK, K32 & K. Y Bty retaliating on ETNA, K26d with 4 rounds Z Bty fires 5 6.6" rounds on enemy's wire at Southern corner of SPOIL HEAP, K20a.	
28		At 2 p.m. Y Bty fires 20 rounds on enemy work at WIGAN, K26d & at 8 p.m. put 5 rounds into WIGAN COPSE on enemy reported to be there. The wire in front of SPOIL HEAP, K20d was damaged with 52 6-inch rounds by Z Bty.	
29		Z Bty fires 28 6" rounds on enemy wire at Southern corner of SPOIL HEAP & 2 2-inch rounds on enemy working party opposite Pt. R3. K26a.	
30		Dirty. Few rounds were exp. on enemy on wire at K33 d 16.30 – K23 d 10 A.M. Two gaps were cut both from 10 to 15 yards wide. Cut 11.30 A.M.	

Army Form C. 2118.

WAR DIARY
or
INTELLIGENCE SUMMARY.
(Erase heading not required.)

Instructions regarding War Diaries and Intelligence Summaries are contained in F.S. Regs., Part II. and the Staff Manual respectively. Title pages will be prepared in manuscript.

Place	Date	Hour	Summary of Events and Information	Remarks and references to Appendices
Dues	1914 30th Cants		2/ Bty expended 14 rounds on wire East of WIGAN, K.26.d. & 2 Bty fires 46 rounds of 6" ammunition on Enemy wire at N.W. edge of SPOIL HEAP, K.20.a.5.1	9
	31.		At 10 a.m. fires 19 rounds on wire just east of DEAN COPSE, K.30.6 at request of the Infantry.	
	2.11.19			A.F. Grisdale Captain, R.F.A. D.T.M.O., 36th Division

Army Form C. 2118.

WAR DIARY
or
INTELLIGENCE SUMMARY. 36th Divisional T.M. Batteries

(Erase heading not required.)

Instructions regarding War Diaries and Intelligence Summaries are contained in F. S. Regs., Part II. and the Staff Manual respectively. Title pages will be prepared in manuscript.

Place	Date 1917	Hour	Summary of Events and Information	Remarks and references to Appendices
Tries	Nov 3.		Hostile artillery became more active than usual on front in the vicinity of YORKSHIRE BANK, K.32 a & c. X Bty fires ten 6" bombs in registration on K.33 b 22.58 & K.33 b 40.10.	
		from 2.30 p.m. to 3 p.m.	V Bty fires 15 rounds from short range mortar & 10 rounds from long-range mortar, with BOGGART'S HOLE as target. The enemy retaliates with 3 rounds from a heavy T.M. on our long-range gun at YORKSHIRE BANK, & with 10 rounds from a heavy Minenwerfer on "E" Sap & our position; no serious damage was done.	
	4.	At 8.30 p.m.	V Bty fires 4 rounds from a long-range T.M. on VESUVIUS in support of a raid made by the 9th Royal Irish Fusiliers. The enemy uses his heavy Minenwerfer in retaliation, & fires 15 cm. & MM. m.m. guns with a few gas shells on MORTAR VALLEY. X Bty	

Army Form C. 2118.

WAR DIARY
or
INTELLIGENCE SUMMARY.
(Erase heading not required.)

Instructions regarding War Diaries and Intelligence Summaries are contained in F. S. Regs., Part II. and the Staff Manual respectively. Title pages will be prepared in manuscript.

Place	Date	Hour	Summary of Events and Information	Remarks and references to Appendices
Dicks	Nov 1914 4 Cont²		fires 12 rounds at hostile T.M. "PANT", scoring a direct hit on Emplacement at K 33 b 40.40. At 6.10 a.m. Z Battery fires 20 rounds from hollow at heads of TALLY-HO LANE, formerly known as ULSTER AVENUE.	
	6.		Y Battery fires 20 rounds at wire about K 33 a 20.25. It was difficult to estimate the area of wire cut, but a fair percentage of rounds fell in the wire. At 2.30 P.M. BOGGART'S HOLE was engaged with 26 heavy bombs by V Battery. During the night Y Battery engages three rounds in ETNA, silencing a machine gun, as well as dispersing a working party at WIGAN COPSE.	
	9.		X Battery fires 15 rounds on wire at K 20.c 60.40 & Y Bty registers a 6-inch T.M. with 10 rounds.	

WAR DIARY
INTELLIGENCE SUMMARY
(Erase heading not required.)

Place	Date	Hour	Summary of Events and Information	Remarks and references to Appendices
Trees	Nov 1917 / 11		Wire cutting was carried out at K.20.c.60.70 by X Bty. Fifty-five 6" bombs being expended. As retaliation to 6 medium Minenwerfer, V Bty fires 5 rounds from long-range gun on VESUVIUS. X Bty expends 20 rounds on wire at K.20.c.53.86, a gap 12 yards wide being made. Z Bty also carries out a wire-cutting shoot with an expenditure of 84 bombs. The enemy retaliates vigorously & scores two direct hits on one of our emplacements, & a direct hit on a second emplacement.	
	12		As covering fire to 2" T.M's V Bty's HERMIES long-range mortar fires 4 rounds on the SLAGG HEAP. X Bty expends 15 rounds on wire at K.20.c.53.84, & Z Bty 35 rounds on the wire at K.14.b.05.35. Heavy retaliation was made by the enemy, who obtained two direct hits on one of our emplacements.	

Army Form C. 2118.

WAR DIARY
or
INTELLIGENCE SUMMARY.
(Erase heading not required.)

IV

Place	Date	Hour	Summary of Events and Information	Remarks and references to Appendices
dies	1917 Nov 13.		With an expenditure of 50 rounds X Bty cut a large gap in wire at K.20.c.50.90. At 4 p.m. Y Bty notices smoke coming out of trench at K.26.d.50.88 & fires 4 rounds at this point, the fire being extinguishes after the third round. A successful wire-cutting shoot of 55 rounds was carried out by Z Bty.	
	14.		Y Bty fires 14 rounds at junction of Sap-heads at K.26.d.70.90. will good effect. Z Bty expends 65 rounds on wire in front of SKAGG STREET.	
	15.		The wire at K.21.c.00.32 & K.24.a.00.95 was bombarded with 64 rounds by X Bty, while Z Bty fires 113 rounds at wire in the vicinity of K.14.b.1.4. Y Bty ranges over its sector, one 6" howitzer, 164 rounds of ammunition & various trench stores to Y/62 T.M. Battery.	
	16.		One long-range howitzer, one short range howitzer & 45 rounds of heavy T.M. ammunition were handed over by V Battery to the 62nd Divisional Artillery. At 2.30 p.m. V Battery fires 19 rounds from	

WAR DIARY or INTELLIGENCE SUMMARY.

Army Form C. 2118.

Place	Date	Hour	Summary of Events and Information	Remarks and references to Appendices
Fins	1917 16th Contd		Long-range mortar on K.24.a.00.50, & Z Battery counters wire as follows: K.24.a.05.32, 40 rounds; K.14.d.92.62, 60 rounds; K.14.b.1.1, 64 rounds.	V
	17.		X Bty fires 106 rounds on wire at K.14.a 79.60 & Z Bty 134 rounds on wire at K.14.b.1.1	
	18.		All Batteries remove from dug-outs in HAVRINCOURT WOOD, P.18.b.0.8 to billets in HERMIES.	
	19.		Twelve men of V Battery were attached to work with field batteries of 153rd & 143rd Bdes. R.F.A. Y Bty fires 60 bombs on wire opposite SKAGG STREET, advantage being taken of this shoot to instruct D.A.C. gunners in the use of the 6" heavy mortar.	
	20.		All mortars remaining at HERMIES. Long-range position (21) were expended by V Bty in support of 3rd Army attack on the HINDENBURG LINE. Two short-range heavies are at TRESCAULT &	

WAR DIARY
or
INTELLIGENCE SUMMARY

Army Form C. 2118.

VI

Place	Date	Hour	Summary of Events and Information	Remarks and references to Appendices
Fins	1917 Nov 20th		Coats and at BUTLER'S CROSS were handed over to the 62nd Divisional Artillery. After the initial portion of the attack the whole of V Bty (less 1 Officer & 6 men) commences constructing tracks on YORKSHIRE BANK. At "Zero plus 135 minutes" the remainder of V Bty went forward to reconnoitre X Bty positions. From 6.30 a.m. to 9.20 a.m. X Bty fires 520 6-inch rounds in barrage on enemy front system. Y Bty expends 604 rounds in conjunction with the general attack, & Z Bty successfully employs 510 6" bombs.	
	21.		X & Y Batteries commence work on ammunition dumps & Z Bty in clearing the DEMICOURT - GRAINCOURT Roads of wire, & filling in trenches.	
	22.		Three officers of V Bty, with 15 N.C.O.'s & men, overseers to captures 77 m/m guns with good effect. Z Bty commences work on an ammunition dump from turn the enemy's guns, succeeding in firing about 460 rounds from	

WAR DIARY
or
INTELLIGENCE SUMMARY

Army Form C. 2118.

Place	Date	Hour	Summary of Events and Information	Remarks and references to Appendices
Fins	1917			
	23 & 24.		The use of captured guns by V Bty was continued. More batteries of 77 m.m. guns were found & from these a considerable number of rounds were fires. V Bty also furnished men for working on an ammunition dump.	
	25 & 26.		Further captures Batteries were put into action by V Bty, including 77 m.m. & 150 m.m. howitzers at positions: K.12.a 30.70 & K.10d 40.70. Some 250 or 300 rounds were disposes of.	
	27.		A 120 m.m. gun at K.12 d 70.10 was brought into action & was used with success by V Bty, & a gun of the same calibre was also used at K.13 a 50.90.	
	28.		Further firing with 120 m.m. guns by V Bty was carried out on FONTAINE & the ridge behind this place.	
	29.		Two ammunition dumps were handed over to the 2nd Divisional Artillery & X, Y & Z Batteries removed from HERMIES to billets at RUYAULCOURT	

Army Form C. 2118.

WAR DIARY
or
INTELLIGENCE SUMMARY.
(Erase heading not required.)

VIII

Instructions regarding War Diaries and Intelligence Summaries are contained in F. S. Regs., Part II. and the Staff Manual respectively. Title pages will be prepared in manuscript.

Place	Date	Hour	Summary of Events and Information	Remarks and references to Appendices
Diels	1919 Nov 30th		V Battery were engaged in making preparations to remove from the neighbourhood of our old line.	
		1.12.M.		

A Gunson
Captain, R.A.
D.T.M.O., 36th Division

Army Form C. 2118.

WAR DIARY
or
INTELLIGENCE SUMMARY. 36th Divisional T.M. Batteries
(Erase heading not required.)

Place	Date	Hour	Summary of Events and Information	Remarks and references to Appendices
	Dec 1917			
	1-4		X, Y & Z Batteries were billeted in RUYAULCOURT & were engaged in work on ammunition dumps at RUYAULCOURT & HERNIES. V Bty. billeted in HERNIES until the 5th, were occupied in work at HERNIES ammunition Dump.	
	5th		V battery removes from HERNIES to RUYAULCOURT.	
	8th		See Batteries removes in G.L. wagons from RUYAULCOURT to METZ.	
	9th		A party of 6 other men from Z/36th battery commences work on gun positions in R.9.a., Sheet 57 C, N.E.2.	
	10th		X Battery commences digging positions on WELSH RIDGE, R.9., Sheet 57 C, N.E.2.	
	14th		Work at WELSH RIDGE positions was completed by X Bty. & mortars were got into action.	

Army Form C. 2118.

WAR DIARY
or
INTELLIGENCE SUMMARY.
(Erase heading not required.)

Instructions regarding War Diaries and Intelligence
Summaries are contained in F. S. Regs., Part II.
and the Staff Manual respectively. Title pages
will be prepared in manuscript.

Place	Date	Hour	Summary of Events and Information	Remarks and references to Appendices
Trees	1914 Dec 18th		One officer & two detachments from Z/36 took over X Bty position.	
	19th		V Battery took over One Lung range 9.45" T.M. & two short-range 9.45" T.M. from the 20th Division	
	20th		Y Battery took over from 20th Division 4 Hows in VILLERS PLOUICH & three guns firing on LA VACQUERIE.	
	21st		Three detachments of Y/36 Bty carries up bombs to dumps. One detachment stood-to all night in shelter in Kaufort Trench & the other two slept in Bucquoi in Sunken Trench.	
	22nd		Drew 6.30 a.m to 7.30 a.m. Y Battery stood-to & at 3pm fires 30 6-inch bombs on Copse Wood in LA VACQUERIE. The enemys artillery was kept active on trenches & on VILLERS PLOUICH	
	23rd		X Battery relieves Z Battery in action.	

Army Form C. 2118.

WAR DIARY
or
INTELLIGENCE SUMMARY.
(Erase heading not required.)

Instructions regarding War Diaries and Intelligence Summaries are contained in F. S. Regs., Part II. and the Staff Manual respectively. Title pages will be prepared in manuscript.

III

Place	Date	Hour	Summary of Events and Information	Remarks and references to Appendices
Dies	1917 Dec 24th		Hostile shelling of trenches was very severe, received very heavy bombardment starting from 6.30 a.m. to 9.30 a.m.	
	25th		Y Battery were relieved in the line by 1/65 Battery & V Battery handed over there 9.45" T. No 6 to the 63rd Division	
	26th		All Batteries entrained at YPRES for CORBIE which town was reached at about 10 p.m.	
	27th		The Batteries remained in hotel lorries to HAMELET & remained there in rest until the end of the month.	

3.1.18.

R. Stranston
Captain R.O.A.
S.T.M.O., 36th Division.

Army Form C. 2118.

WAR DIARY
or
INTELLIGENCE SUMMARY. 36th Div: Trench Mortar Batteries

(Erase heading not required.)

Instructions regarding War Diaries and Intelligence Summaries are contained in F. S. Regs., Part II. and the Staff Manual respectively. Title pages will be prepared in manuscript.

Place	Date	Hour	Summary of Events and Information	Remarks and references to Appendices
Divs.	1918 Jany			
	1-6		All Batteries were billeted in the rest area of HAMELET, near CORBIE, where training was carried out.	
	7th		The Batteries marched from HAMELET to LE QUESNEL, stores & kits being conveyed by motor lorries.	
	11th		X/36 & V/36 Batteries marches to ROYE. Y/36 & Z/36 Batteries proceeded in lorries to GRAND SERAUCOURT, & commenced work the same night at an ammunition dump in that village.	
	13th		X/36 & V/36 Batteries travelled in lorries from ROYE to GRAND SERAUCOURT.	
	15th		X/36, Y/36 & Z/36 Batteries took over from the French in front of ST. QUENTIN, & commenced work on new positions for 2" T.M.s. V Battery was employed in renovating billets, quarrying dug-outs in the line, & work at GRAND SERAUCOURT ammunition dump.	
	16-31st		The Medium Batteries were engaged in the construction of 2" positions	

Army Form C. 2118.

WAR DIARY
or
INTELLIGENCE SUMMARY.
(Erase heading not required.)

II

Place	Date	Hour	Summary of Events and Information	Remarks and references to Appendices
Diels	1918 Jan'y 16-31st		& the repair & revetting of trenches. Eight 2" T.M.s. (taken over from the 36th Division) were got into action & 245 rounds of ammunition carried to the positions. V Battery removed from billets at GRAND SERAUCOURT to dug-outs nearer the line.	
	20th			
	21-31st		Work on the various positions, trenches, etc., was continued by X, Y & Z Batteries. V Battery was engaged in constructing extra 18-pr positions for the 173rd Bde, R.F.A., & additional dug-outs for the accommodation of the Battery, besides repairing gun-pits to be used for 9.45" T.M.s.	

R.H. [Signature]
Captain, R.A.
D.T.M.O., 36th Division.

D.T.M.O.,
36th DIVISION.
1.2.18

WAR DIARY
or
INTELLIGENCE SUMMARY.
(Erase heading not required.)

Army Form C. 2118.

36th Divisional Trench Mortar Batteries for the month of February.

Place	Date	Hour	Summary of Events and Information	Remarks and references to Appendices
	1-8th		Working on positions in forward area	
	9.10		Building positions in S P line and Battle Zone.	
	11th		Trench Mortar Batteries reorganised.	
	12-28th		Carried on with positions in SP line and Battle Zone.	

D.T.M.O. [signature] Capt R.A
36th DIVISION.
DTMO 36. Division

36th Divisional Artillery.

TRENCH MORTAR OFFICER

36th DIVISION.

MARCH 1918

C O N F I D E N T I A L. 36th Div. G.X. 20/462

D. A. G.
   3rd Echelon.

     With reference to your G.R. No. 140/452 dated 26th July, the War Diary of the Divl. T.M. Batteries for the Month of March 1918 is forwarded herewith.

                                    Major-General,

29. 7. 18.   Commanding 36th Division.

36

MARCH 1918
36th DIVISIONAL TRENCH MORTARS
WAR DIARY
or
INTELLIGENCE SUMMARY.
(Erase heading not required.)

Army Form C. 2118.

Appx VI 21

Place	Date	Hour	Summary of Events and Information	Remarks and references to Appendices
	1st–20th 1/3/18		From 1/3/18 to 20/3/18 x T. 7/36 T.M. Batteries were occupying defensive positions covering 36th Divisional front in ST. QUENTIN Sector. One battery manned S.P. line maintaining 3 sections in action as under.	
			JEANNE D'ARC — 2 T.Ms.	
			GRUGIES Railway Cutting 2 T.Ms.	
			BOADICEA — 2 T.Ms.	
			One battery manned the Battle line, maintaining 3 sections in action. Billets for this battery were in SERAUCOURT.	
	21st		(For March 21st. See official report attached)	
	22–31		Remaining personnel were attached to 36. D.A.C. and carried out work on ammunition dumps.	

N. Fox
Captain
D.T.M.O. 36th Division

TRENCH MORTARS.

March 21st.

The only Medium Trench Mortar Operations known on this date are as follows :

FORWARD ZONE. There were 2 6" newton Mortars in each of the Strong Points, manned by detachments from Y/36th Trench Mortar Battery. Scarcely any information as to what happened to these detachments can be obtained. Owing to the thick mist the enemy were practically into the Right Strong Point 'JEANNE D'ARC' before being discovered. As the Officer in charge of the Mortars was last seen running into the emplacement it is probably that a number of rounds were fired before the Strong Point was taken.

The Centre Strong Point at GRUGIES was attacked in the rear and an Infantryman reports that the enemy were bombing the Trench Mortar dugouts as he escaped. As to whether the Mortars were fired he could not say.

Regarding the Left Strong Point nothing is known.

BATTLE ZONE. The Mortars in the Battle Zone were manned by X/36th Trench Mortar Battery. One Mortar was situated on the Railway embankment at A.30.c.7.3. Sheet 66 C N.W. The Officer in charge here was killed early in the bombardment in his O.P. The enemy were close to the emplacement before being seen and the Sergeant in charge was killed immediately afterwards. Two rounds were fired. One of the detachment escaped.

Two Mortars were in an emplacement in the bank of the roadway at A.29.c.7.4. The enemy first appeared here in front of the wire about 300 yards away at 11.45 a.m. Fire was immediately opened on the Valleys in A.23.c. and d. in accordance with the barrage table. After 40 rounds were expended, one Mortar went out of action. By this time parties of the enemy were visible from the emplacement so fire was directed on these until ammunition was expended. Altogether 113 rounds were fired from this position. The Mortars were taken back to a trench held by our Infantry and buried in the parados A.29.c.62.41.

Two Mortars were in the Sunken Road at A.28.c.6.2. These were fired till hard pressed by the enemy, when the detachments retired at the order of the Officer in command of V/18th Heavy Trench Mortars, their own Officer having by this time been severely wounded. Seventy five rounds were fired and the Mortars were partially destroyed before the position was abandoned.

One Mortar was in the Keep in A.20.a. This gun first came into action about 3.0 p.m. on the 21st March. The enemy by this time were advancing on this part of the battle line from the HAM - ST. QUENTIN Road in A.2. and A.3.and beginning to occupy the Sunken Roads in A.14. also FONTAINE. On this occasion 30 rounds were fired in the barrage line (Valley in A.14.) and as far right as the bed would allow. From then and during the night the enemy made no further advance except down the bank of the Canal, but about 6.30 a.m. on the 22nd an intense and accurate machine gun fire was directed on the whole position from much closer than on the previous evening, and also from the Canal Bank as far down as A.20.c.50.50. Three S.O.S. Rockets were sent up by the Infantry, but the thick mist rendered them invisible from any distance. The remaining rounds (50) were then fired from this Mortar on the barrage line and up to $20°$ more Left at a rate of 2 a minute. The gun was finally dismounted and taken back to Battalion Headquarters and the clinometer removed.

36th Divisional Artillery.

X & Y TRENCH MROTAR BATTERIES

36th DIVISION.

APRIL 1918.

WAR DIARY
X & Y NT. Btys. 36 DIV ART

PLACE	DATE	
LA RUE ST PIERRE	1/4/18	Moved into Reserve in Huts with DAC
AUCHY LANDRINGHEM	2/4/18	Marched with DAC to Auchy & Mortagne
CHARNY	3/4/18	Marched with DAC to G Army
"	4/4/18	Drawing rifles & ammunition & necessaries & rules & consols
"	5/4/18	Cleaning up
"	6/4/18	Doing fatigues for DAC
"	7/4/18	/do
COURSELLES	8/4/18	Marched with DAC to Coursellés
"	9/4/18	Awaiting orders
"	10/4/18	/do
PONT-à-METZ	11/4/18	Marched to Pont de Metz
"	12 & 13/4/18	Doing fatigues for DAC
"	14/4/18	X Bty moved with No 2 Sect & Y with No 1 Sect DAC to St Roch Station and entrained for Poperinghe siding

PLACE	DATE	
GODEWAERSVELDE	18/4/18	Entrained at HOPOUTRE & marched to GODEWAERSVELDE
"	19/4/18	Cleaning up
"	20/4/18	Foot & rifle drill. Instruction to NCOs on LEWIS GUN
"	21/4/18	Rifle drill
"	22/4/18	
"	23/4/18	Drill and fatigues.
HAMHOEK	24/4/18	Marched to HAMHOEK STAIDINGS
PESELHOEK	25/4/18	Marched to PESELHOEK STAIDINGS
"	26/4/18	Doing fatigues for RAC
"	27/4/18	do
"	28/4/18	
"	29/4/18	Party employed burying two 20 horses of 9/173 RFA killed by shell fire
"	30/4/18	Turned woodwork fatigues

S. Withers Major RFA
OC X/36 TMB
5/5/18

36 Divisional Trench Mortar Batteries

MAY 1918

WAR DIARY or INTELLIGENCE SUMMARY

Army Form C. 2118.

REF. SHEET 28 NW   1 - 20,000

Vol 2

Place	Date MAY	Hour	Summary of Events and Information	Remarks and references to Appendices
PESELHOEK	1st.		1 Officer, 20 O.Rs. from X/36. T.M.B. } detached on Remount Conducting Duty	
	2nd } 3rd		12 O.Rs. " " Y/36. T.M.B. }	
	4th.		Working Parties provided to Units	
			Remount parties returned from D.A.C. 36th Div.	
			1 N.C.O., 5 O.Rs. from Y/36. } detached for work on Ammunition Dumps	
			5 O.Rs. " X/36. }	
	5th.		Working Parties provided for 36th D.A.C.	
	6th.		" " " "	
			Lieut. R. M. MACNAMARA X/36. Returned to duty from Hospital	
	7th.		Working Parties provided for 36th D.A.C	
			Lieut. H. M. BRETON. Posted to Y/36. T.M.B	
	8th		X/36. received six 6-inch T.M. from Ordnance.	
	9th.		2 H. O.Rs. Posted to Y/36. as reinforcements.	
			6 O.Rs. " " X/36. " "	
	10th.		1 NCO. 6 O.Rs. X/36. attached to 173rd Brigade. R.F.A. for Original instruction	
			1 NCO. 6 O.Rs. Y/36. " " 153rd " " " "	
			" " " " 152nd " " " "	

Army Form C. 2118.

36th Div. T.M. Batteries.

WAR DIARY or INTELLIGENCE SUMMARY
(Erase heading not required.)

Ref. Sheet. 28 N.W. 1:20,000

Place	Date	Hour	Summary of Events and Information	Remarks and references to Appendices
C.25.c.9.9.	12th		1 Officer + 20 O.Rs. X/36. } moved into dugouts at about C.25.c.9.9.	
			" + 25 O.Rs. Y/36. }	
			2/Lieut. A.G.S. GOSLING. R.F.A. Posted to Y/36. from 152nd Brigade R.F.A.	
			2/Lieut. J.J. THOMPSON. R.F.A. Posted to X/36. " 143rd "	
			1 O.R. Posted to Y/36. 1 O.R. Posted to X/36.	
	13th		X/36. T.M.B. started work on constructing at C.22.d.9.5 (T.B. Zero 106°).	
			Y/36. " " " " - C.22.b.52.10 (T.B. Zero 60°)	
	14th		- - - defensive Positions at I.1.t.6.4. { T.B. Rt. Gun. 100°	
				T.B. Lt. Gun. 50° }
			X/36 - - - at C.25.d.1.6 (T.B. Zero 106°)	
			Y/36 - - - - - - -	
	15th 16- 17th		Work continued on all Positions	
	18th		Bombardier. C. W. CORBETT. awarded "Military Medal" Authy. R.A.D.O. 216.b.a. 14-5-18	
			No. 3 Sections of Batteries relieved No. 1 Sections in line	
			2/Lieut. S.T. HAZELL Posted to X/36. T.M.B. from 143rd Brigade R.F.A.	
			" " " " " " - Y/36 - - 152 - " "	
			Lieut. D.W. DAVEY - - - Y/36 - - - - - - -	
			2/Lieut. " Posted to "	

36th Div T.M. Batteries

Army Form C. 2118.

Instructions regarding War Diaries and Intelligence Summaries are contained in F.S. Regs., Part II. and the Staff Manual respectively. Title pages will be prepared in manuscript.

WAR DIARY
or
INTELLIGENCE SUMMARY.
(Erase heading not required.)

Place	Date	Hour	Summary of Events and Information	Remarks and references to Appendices
SHEET 28 N.W. 1/20.000	19th		X/36. T.M.B. started work on defensive Position in Belgian Army Area about C.19.a.05.60. (T.B. Zero 135°).	
	20th		Work continued on all Positions	
	21st		Y/36. started work on Position at I.H.a.4.9. (T.B. Zero 74°).	
			X/36. took over from Y/36 Position at { C.22.d.52.10. / C.25.d.10.60.	
			Y/36. " " " X/36. - I.1.t.6.4.	
	22nd		T.M.B. in action at following Positions { C.22.d.52.10. 1 Gun. / C.22.d.9.5. 1 " / I.1.t.6.4. 2 "s.	
			600 rounds T.M.G. received.	
			Code names allotted to Positions as under & hereafter used.	
			I.H.a.4.9. (Y/36.) — GAIETY	
			C.22.d.9.5. (X/36.) — TIVOLI	
			C.22.b.5.1 (X/36.) — DALYS	
			I.1.t.6.4. (Y/36.) — {R.LOCKHART'S / L.A.B.C}	
			C.25.d.1.6 (X/36.) — PRINCE'S	Forward Positions
			C.19.a.05.60 (Y/36.) — MONICO	Defensive Positions for CANAL LINE

Army Form C. 2118.

36th Div. T.M. Batteries.

WAR DIARY
or
INTELLIGENCE SUMMARY.
(Erase heading not required.)

Instructions regarding War Diaries and Intelligence Summaries are contained in F.S. Regs., Part II. and the Staff Manual respectively. Title pages will be prepared in manuscript.

(4)

Place	Date	Hour	Summary of Events and Information	Remarks and references to Appendices
Ref Sheet. 28. N.W. 1.20.000.	23rd.	11 a.m.	X/36. fired 6 rounds on UHLAN FARM. from TIVOLI in registration	
		10.30 p.m.	" " 10 " " " " in retaliation for hostile T.M.s	
	24th		Rest Camp A 21.a.4.8. shelled by H.V. guns. Work continued on all positions.	
	25		GAIETY. in action.	
	26th		2 inter-section relief carried out – T.M. in action at MONICO. 1 O.R. wounded by hostile shell fire – 1 O.R. left to attend Gas. Course 1/Lieut (a/Capt) J.CUTHBERT. RFA. attached. X/36. T.M.B. awarded "Military Cross" Autty R.G.D.O. 2181 dated 26.5.18	
	27th 3.0 p.m.		X/36. fired 6 rounds on JASPER FARM. from TIVOLI in retaliation	
	28th 5.0 p.m.		" " 4 " " CHEDDAR.VILLA " DALYS "	
	11.0 p.m. to 11.40 p.m.		DALYS & TIVOLI. in support of operation by our infantry. + BOSSAERT. KEEP from BOSSAERT. KEEP.	
	29th 2.30 a.m.		X/36. fired 12 rounds on BOSSAERT. KEEP. from DALYS in retaliation Y/36. " 12 " " UHLAN KEEP. " TIVOLI " " " 6 " " C.29.C.7.5. " GAIETY " "	

WAR DIARY or INTELLIGENCE SUMMARY

Army Form C. 2118.

36th Divl. T.M. Batteries

Place	Date	Hour	Summary of Events and Information	Remarks and references to Appendices
28.N.W. 1/20.000	29/5		X/36. T.M.B. started work on defensive positions at A.24.b.1.4. Y/36. " " " " " A.24.c.9.1. Lieut H.M. BRETON admitted to Hospital sick.	
	30th		Inter-section relief carried out.	
	31st		X/36. fired 2 rounds on BOSSAERT KEEP from DALY'S in retaliation. 1 O.R. wounded by H.S. fire.	

Total Casualties 2 O.R.

J.W. Fa__
Captain
W. Rid. Regt.
D.T.M.O., 36th Divn.
1.6.18.

WAR DIARY
~~INTELLIGENCE SUMMARY~~

(*Erase heading not required.*)

Army Form C. 2118.

Vol 24

36th. Divisional. T. M. Batteries.

WAR DIARY   JUNE 1918

REF. SHEET 28 N.W.
            27 N.E.

WAR DIARY
or
INTELLIGENCE SUMMARY

Army Form C. 2118.

(Erase heading not required.)

Place	Date	Hour	Summary of Events and Information	Remarks and references to Appendices

At the beginning of the month both batteries were in line covering the 36th Divisional front in the WIELTJE sector;

1/1 Battery covering the Right Sub-section under 153 Brigade R.F.A.
X/1 Battery " " " Left " " 149 " R.F.A.

2 sections of each battery were in line and one section in rest at PESELHOEK.

Distribution of mortars was as follows:-

FORWARD.- 1 T.M. at 15.a.50.85. 1 T.M. at C.23.d.82.32. 1 T.M. at C.19.d.05.41

CANAL LINE - 2 T.M's on each Brigade front.

Resting. - 5 T.M's.

Work was proceeding on Divisions in reserve lines of defence as under:-

BRANDHOEK. (YELLOW) Line - H Position
E POPERINGHE (BLUE) Line - H Position

WAR DIARY
or
INTELLIGENCE SUMMARY.
(Erase heading not required.)

Army Form C. 2118.

Place	Date	Hour	Summary of Events and Information	Remarks and references to Appendices
			The amount TMs expended on active duties of retaliation for hostile TMs fire, which eventually ceased almost entirely. Fire was also given in support of minor operations, & TMs were manned permanently for S.O.S. purposes. A total of 290 rounds was fired during the month. On the 4th inst, 36 Div. Arty handed over command of WIELTJE sector to 12th C.A.D.I. Belgian Army. 36 H Div T.M.Bs. remained in line under orders of 12th C.A.D.I. subsequently of 8th C.A.D.I. until their withdrawal for rest training on 24th, 28th of the month to PALMER CAMP in the PROVEN Area. The same general duties was maintained under Belgian Army, but distribution of personnel was changed, one battery completely being kept in line & one in rest.	

D.T.M.O. 36th DIVISION.   Lieut (a/Captain) L. W. FOX. M.C. W. RIDING. REGT. T.C.
O.C. x/36. T.M.Bty.   Lieut (a/Captain) J. CUTHBERT. M.C.   R.F.A. (T.C.)
O.C. y/36. T.M.Bty.   Lieut (a/Captain) L. N. VINEN. M.C.   R.F.A. (T.C.)

Army Form C. 2118.

WAR DIARY
or
INTELLIGENCE SUMMARY.
(Erase heading not required.)

Place	Date	Hour	Summary of Events and Information	Remarks and references to Appendices
Ref Sheet 28 T.M.	June 5.			
	1		10 a.m. continued in all positions DALYS, TIVOLI completed	
			7/36. T.M.B. fired 4 rounds on MILL COT from GAIETY in registration	
	2		Later sections which carried out	
		2 a.m.	7/36. fired 6 rounds on MINNIE FRITZ from GAIETY in retaliation	
		4.50 a.m.	x/36. " 11 " " CHEDDAR VILLA " DALYS as covering fire for raiding party	
		2.0.a	x/36. " 3 " " RAT KEEP " " " in retaliation	
		4.0 a.m.	-/36. " 2 " " MINNIE FRITZ " GAIETY for hostile T.M.	
	5	4.0 a.m.	x/36. " 18 " " CHEDDAR VILLA " DALYS in retaliation	
		4.0.	x/36. " 4 " " UHLAN KEEP " TIVOLI " "	
			2 " 2 Officers and 22 Ranks. proceeded to II Army T.M. School for course of instruction	
			Headquarters section was moved to HIRST CAMP A9 d 9.2	
	6	6.45 a.m.	7/36. fired 10 rounds on MINNIE FRITZ from GAIETY in retaliation	
			100 clubs T.M.G. received	

Army Form C. 2118.

WAR DIARY
or
INTELLIGENCE SUMMARY.
(Erase heading not required.)

Instructions regarding War Diaries and Intelligence Summaries are contained in F. S. Regs., Part II. and the Staff Manual respectively. Title pages will be prepared in manuscript.

Place	Date June	Hour	Summary of Events and Information	Remarks and references to Appendices
Pop Stub	7.		Inter relieve carried out — 36 H. D.H. relieved by 12 H. CADI Belgian Army. 36 H. T.M.Bs remained in line	
	8.		D.T.M.O moved this H.Qrs to HIRST CAMP on previous continued "PRINCES" completed. Bdr. J.K. ROBERTSON granted leave to U.K.	
	9.	2.15 a.m.	X/36 fired 5 rounds on CHEDDAR VILLA from DALYS in retaliation	
		7.0 p.m.	Y/36 " 8 " " MILL COT " " verification of registration	
		6.4.30.	Y/36 " 10 " " WARWICK FARM " " " "	
	10.	12.30 a.m.	X/36. " 3 " " CHEDDAR VILLA in retaliation	
	11.		-/36. Lieut H. M¢BRETON returning to duty from hospital. Capt. H. Qrs on Canal Bank West. -/36. complete moved into reel. H. Qrs at HIRST CAMP & continued BLUE & YELLOW reserve line function	
	12.	2.20 a.m.	Y/36 fired 4 rounds on CHEDDAR VILLA from DALYS in retaliation continued work on all function	
	13.		-/36. fired 2 rounds on CHEDDAR VILLA from DALYS to verify registration	
	14.		-/36. " 20 " " from C.14.c.45.25 to CHEDDAR VILLA — in support of operation	
	15.		Gas Emission "PALACE" started at C.99.d.85.30 to cover Right Regtl Front 12 H. D.I.	
	16.		Continued work on all function	

WAR DIARY
or
INTELLIGENCE SUMMARY
(Erase heading not required.)

Army Form C. 2118.

Place	Date	Hour	Summary of Events and Information	Remarks and references to Appendices
Potijze 98 Y.W.	Oct 17		GAIETY position with 4 obs. Ammunition handed over to 49th Div. T.M.B. PALACE position in action for Retaliation. T.B. OS. 7/36 received 5 reinforcements 7/36 received 4.	
	18		7/36 fired 15 rounds on C.19 d 20.62 from DALYS } in support of infantry 15 " C.23 d 90.10 " TIVOLI raid at C.23 d.10.35	
	19		X/36 relieved 7/36 in line	
	20		Work on all positions continued.	
	21	11.15 p.m.	X/36 fired 2 rounds on PAT. KEEP from TIVOLI in retaliation 7 " " KHAAN KEEP " " 3 " " BOSSAERT FARM " DALYS "	
	22	12.30 a.m. to 2.30 a.m.	12th CADI relieved by 8th CADI. – Lieut A.M.BRETON handed over to U.K. X/36 fired 9 rounds on JASPER FARM " TIVOLI in retaliation 6 " " C.23 d.7.1 " " 3 " " JASPER FARM " " 2 " " " " "	
	23		Work on all positions continued – Lieut A.P.BUCHANAN posted from 153rd Bde R.F.A.	
	24	9.30 a.m. 1.30 p.m.	X/36. fired 4 rounds on CHEDDAR VILLA " DALYS in retaliation 5 " " JASPER FARM " PALACE " Lieut J.M. BRETON 9 handed over to U.K. on augmentation	

Army Form C. 2118.

WAR DIARY
or
INTELLIGENCE SUMMARY.
(Erase heading not required.)

Instructions regarding War Diaries and Intelligence Summaries are contained in F.S. Regs., Part II. and the Staff Manual respectively. Title pages will be prepared in manuscript.

Place	Date	Hour	Summary of Events and Information	Remarks and references to Appendices
Shk 28 N.W.	25.		Quiet day. Continued work on position. 2/Lieut- S.T. HAZELL returned to duty from Hospital	
	26	4 am	X/36 fired 24 rounds on JASPER FARM from DALYS } in retaliation and	
		4.30 pm	" " 14 " " RAT KEEP " TIVOLI } destruction shoots	
		2.30 am	" " 8 " " UHLAN KEEP " DALYS " in retaliation	
		3.0 -	" " 10 " " BOSSHERT KEEP " DALYS "	
			All wounds in CANAL LINE sent down by Lt Railway to F.A. DUMP	
			TMS in CANAL LINE taken out of action	
	27.		X/Bty fired 24 rounds on JASPER KEEP from PALACE } in retaliation +	
			" " 24 " " RAT KEEP - TIVOLI } destruction shoot	
			Y/Bty relief + Bty in line. Relief cancelled & under orders from	
			36 It D.A. Lt Bty batteries, with all TMS and stores moved out of line	
			to HIRST CAMP. by Lt Railway	
			BDR S. CROUCHER granted leave to U.K.	
Shk 24 N.E.	28		Bty batteries + D.T.M.O moved by Lt Railway to Rest + Training	
			at PALMER CAMP. E.18.d.2.2.	
	29.		Unit all day fitting out Camp.	
	30.		Fatigues on camp + gun. emp.	

Total Casualties Nil

N Fox
Captain
DTMO 36th DIVISION

A.5834 Wt. W4973/M687 750,000 8/16 D.D. & L. Ltd. Forms/C.2118/13.

Army Form C. 2118.

WAR DIARY
or
INTELLIGENCE SUMMARY.
(Erase heading not required.)

Vol 25

36th DIVISIONAL T.M. BATTERIES

JULY. 1918

WAR DIARY

REF SHEET 28
" 27

WAR DIARY
or
INTELLIGENCE SUMMARY.
(Erase heading not required.)

Army Form C. 2118.

At the beginning of the month both batteries were in rest at Palmer Camps, in the Proven Area, moving subsequently to the Hardelot Area, near CASSEL where they remained till the 8th of the month. During this period, mostly, Gas training were carried out. On the 6th & 7th of the month the 36th Division took over the St JAMES CAPPEL Sector from the Rigth Divn XVI French Corps becoming Rigth Division I Corps, on the 8th a reconnoitring Party of 36th T.M.Bs moved forward to P.A.H.Q. MONT.DES.CATS. and remaining Personnel moved forward to ST SILVESTRE CAPPEL. On completion of reconnaissance batteries moved into billets at Pot-des-Pots. Work throughout the month was confined to construction of Provisions for defence of the 3rd & BLUE defensive systems, no offensive work being undertaken X/36.TMB occupied Rigth Sub-Sector. 1/36.TMB the left. By midnight 23rd/24th 12 TMs were in action.

Order of Battle DTMO Lieut (a/Capt) LIONEL WRAY FOX. M.C   WEST.RIDING.REGT.
                        3/Lieut (a/Capt) JOHN CUTHBERT. M.C   RFA
          OCX/36.   3/Lieut (a/Capt) LAWRENCE NORTHCOTT. VINEN. MC RFA

Army Form C. 2118.

WAR DIARY
or
INTELLIGENCE SUMMARY.
(Erase heading not required.)

Instructions regarding War Diaries and Intelligence Summaries are contained in F. S. Regs, Part II. and the Staff Manual respectively. Title pages will be prepared in manuscript.

Place	Date	Hour	Summary of Events and Information	Remarks and references to Appendices
Ref Sheet 28	1.3		Rest & training at Palmer Camp E.18.d.2.2	
	4	8 am	Move by lorries to HARDIFORT (near CASSEL) area I.34.b.7.0	
	5.6		Training continued	
	7		1 O.R. X/Bty to duty from Hospital	
	8	9 am	Move by lorries to ST. SYLVESTRE CAPPEL Q.31.a.1.9	
			D.T.M.O. 1 officer X/36, 1 officer Y/36. to H.Q. R.A – MONT DES CATS. Advance party 10 O.Rs X/36. to MONT. DES CATS	
	9		1 O.R Y/36. to duty from leave	
	10			
	11	8 pm	Remaining personnel move to billets R.21.a.0.8	
			2/Lieut J.T. HAZELL proceeds on leave to U.K.	
	13		Bmgr. of surplus stores left at Q.31.a.1.9 under 1 NCO + 2 O.Rs Reconnaissance completed Positions detailed as under.	

	3rd. Line	No OF GUNS	NAMES – LOCATIONS	ARCS OF FIRE	S.O.S. TARGETS
		2	KOPJE X.5.a.82.12	205° — 95°	(R) X.11.c.5.9 (L) X.11.b.9.5
		2	MULEHOEK M.32.a.45.95	210° — 110°	(R) S.2.b.2.7 (L) S.2.b.90.95

BLUE LINE – see sheet 2.

Army Form C. 2118.

WAR DIARY
or
INTELLIGENCE SUMMARY.
(Erase heading not required.)

Instructions regarding War Diaries and Intelligence Summaries are contained in F. S. Regs., Part II. and the Staff Manual respectively. Title pages will be prepared in manuscript.

Place	Date	Hour	Summary of Events and Information	Remarks and references to Appendices
			BLUE LINE NO OF GUNS NAMES LOCATIONS ARCS OF FIRE	SOS TARGETS
			2 IBEX R 34 c 3.1 175° — 95°	(R) X 5 c 45.45
				(L) X 5 a 5.3
			2 LA MANCHE R 29. c. 70.15 190° — 110°	(R) R 36 c 25.05
				(L) R 36 c 20.45
			2 POT. AU. LAIT R 30 c 80.95 200° — 105°	(R) R 30 c 55.30
				(L) M 32 a 15.35
			2 MONT NOIR M 26 b 20.15 205° — 95°	(R) M 32 a 75.35
				(L) M 33 a 15.45
	14.		2 Sections X/36 to R34 a 8.5 for work on KOPJE	
			2 Section 1/36 — M25 d 4.5 for work on MULEHOEK.	
	16.		X/36 start work on "IBEX" 7/36 start work on POT AU LAIT	
			1 O.R 7/36 proceeds on leave to U.K. — 1 O.R to duty from Hospital	
	17.		IBEX & POT. AU. LAIT in action & manned in view of suspected hostile	
			attack on Dick front. 100 rounds T.M.G per gun received	
	20.		10 carp commenced at LA MANCHE & MONT NOIR positions	
			Rient. A.M. BRETON to duty from leave to U.K.	
			1 O.R proceed on leave — from 7/36.	
	21.		KOPJE & MULEHOEK positions in action & 50 rounds per gun received	
			1 O.R to Second Army T.M. School	

WAR DIARY
or
INTELLIGENCE SUMMARY.
(Erase heading not required.)

Army Form C. 2118.

Place	Date	Hour	Summary of Events and Information	Remarks and references to Appendices
	23		LA MANCHE & POT. AU. LAIT got into action in view of expected hostile attack on Div. front. 200 rounds T.M.G. to LA MANCHE & 100 to MONT NOIR. 3 O.Ps. 1/36. became Casualties through hostile Gas Shelling	
	24		IBEX position destroyed by hostile shell fire. Casualties to personnel — 3 O.Ps. x/36 wounded. " " equipment — NIL. " " ammunition — 200 rounds. T.M.G. destroyed	
	26		100 rounds T.M.G. to POT. AU. LAIT. 1 O.P. 1/36. to duty from leave. Lieut H.M.BRETON to Hospital	
	27		x/36 started work on new IBEX position R34 c 4.4. 1 O.P. posted to x/36. 2 O.Ps. posted to -/36.	
	29		100 rounds T.M.G. to MULEHOEK	
	30		200 " " IBEX. 2 O.Ps. 7/36 to duty from Hospital	
	31		3 O.Ps. posted to x/36. 1 O.P. 7/36. to duty from Hospital	
			Casualties during month —	KILLED WOUNDED W.GAS
			PERSONNEL	NIL 3 3
			EQUIPMENT	NIL

S.W.Fox
Captain
D.T.M.O 36th Division

Army Form C. 2118.

WAR DIARY
or
INTELLIGENCE SUMMARY.

(Erase heading not required.)

36th Divisional T.M. Batteries

WAR DIARY   AUGUST 1918

WAR DIARY
or
INTELLIGENCE SUMMARY

(Erase heading not required.)

Army Form C. 2118.

Place	Date	Hour	Summary of Events and Information	Remarks and references to Appendices

At the opening of this month the dispositions of 36th Div¹ T.M.Bn were as in the previous month. Work was continued throughout the month on strengthening & improving existing defensive positions behind line & Blue line. On the 4th, T.M.H.Q. on MONT DES CATS was 3 times shelled, some casualties being sustained, & H.Q. was moved to R13C2.4 near GODEWAERSVELDE.

Arrangements were made to bring 12 T.M.s into action on the Right Brigade front for wire cutting during the first week of the month, but were cancelled later in the month by a series of short local advances, the Corps front was advanced about 500 yards, throughout a reconnaissance of the captured area was made with a view to bringing T.M.s into action for offensive purposes.

On the night 29/30th the enemy withdrew his lines opposite & unusual front. On the 31st all guns were taken out of action & an officer & party of X/36 were Octd for duty at forward ammunition dumps in ST JANS CAPPEL. Arrangements were being made during the month for construction of special beds & carriages with a view to making experiments to increase the mobility of M.T.Ms.

Order of Battle. D.T.M.O. - Lieut (a/Captain) Lionel. Wray. toy. M.C. West Riding Regt.   Annexed
O.C. X/36. Hospitalised (a/Captain) John Cuthbert. M.C. R.F.A.   ② Defence Scheme
O.C. Y/36. Lieut (a/Captain) Lawrence Northcott. Vivien. M.C. R.F.A.

WAR DIARY
~~INTELLIGENCE SUMMARY.~~
(Erase heading not required.)

Army Form C. 2118.

Instructions regarding War Diaries and Intelligence Summaries are contained in F. S. Regs., Part II. and the Staff Manual respectively. Title pages will be prepared in manuscript.

Place	Date	Hour	Summary of Events and Information	Remarks and references to Appendices
	1		1 O.R. 7/36 returned from leave. — 1 O.R. 7/36 returned to duty from Hospital	
	2		1 " " admitted to Hospital — 1 " " x/36	
	4		H.Q. R.21 a.0.8. shelled at 11 a.m., 1 p.m., & 6 p.m. by H.2 c.m. hows. H.Q. moved to R.13 c.9.4	
	5		1 O.R. x/36 wounded & admitted to Hospital, 2 O.R's " x + 2 O.R's " wounded & remain at duty	
	6		1 O.R. x/36 proceeded on leave to U.K. — 1 O.R. 7/36 admitted to Hospital sick	
	7		1 O.R. 7/36 returned from leave	
	8		1 O.R. x/36 returned to duty from Hospital	
	10		10 O.R's returned from course at I Army. T.M. School — 1 O.R. x/36 to II Army. Cookery School	
	11		Lieut. H.M. Breton. 1/4K Mcr Regt, att. 7/36. T.M.By. struck off the strength	
	12		2/Lieut J.J. Thompson, 5 O.R's x/36 & 4 O.R's 7/36. proceed to I Army. T.M. School	
	13		1 O.R. x/36 proceeded on leave to U.K. — 1 O.R. " x " returned from leave	
	15		1 O.R. x/36 returned from leave	
	16		1 O.R. posted to x/36 from 153rd Brigade R.F.A.	
	18		1 O.R. 7/36 proceeded on leave	
	21		1 O.R. x/36 returned from leave	
	22		1 O.R. x/36 proceeded on leave	

Army Form C. 2118.

WAR DIARY
or
INTELLIGENCE SUMMARY.
(Erase heading not required.)

Instructions regarding War Diaries and Intelligence Summaries are contained in F. S. Regs., Part II. and the Staff Manual respectively. Title pages will be prepared in manuscript.

Place	Date	Hour	Summary of Events and Information	Remarks and references to Appendices
	23		1 OR. posted to X/36 from 36th DAC. — 1 OR. posted from X/36 to 36th DAC	
	25		1 OR. X/36 admitted to Hospital	
	26		1 OR. " returned from leave	
	27		1 OR. " proceeded on leave to U.K.	
	28		2nd Lieut. H. E. Parnell MC. RFA. posted to X/36 from 153rd Brigade. RFA.	
	29		1 OR. X/36 returned from Hospital. Enemy artillery opposite Divisional Front	
	30		1 OR. X/36 proceeded on leave to U.K. 1 OR. X/36 returned from leave. All T.M's taken out of action.	
	31		1 Officer + 10 OR. X/36 TMB to duty at forward Dump. ST. JANS. CAPPEL 1 OR. X/36 returned to duty from Hospital	

Casualties during month. — Killed Wounded
Personnel — Nil 6.
Equipment — Nil

[Signature] Fox, Captain

Army Form C. 2118.

WAR DIARY
or
INTELLIGENCE SUMMARY.
(Erase heading not required.)

WO 27

36th DIVISIONAL T.M. BATTERIES

SEPTEMBER 1918

WAR DIARY

WAR DIARY
~~INTELLIGENCE SUMMARY~~

(Erase heading not required.)

Army Form C. 2118.

Place	Date	Hour	Summary of Events and Information	Remarks and references to Appendices
			At the beginning of the month sections from each battery were employed at forward ammunition dumps, the remaining personnel being attached to 153rd & 143rd Bdes R.F.A. for general purposes. On the 10th inst all personnel rejoined their respective batteries & moved forward to S.12.d.4.6. The following day 1 Officer & 20 men from each battery commenced work on positions for Howitzers in the PLOEGSTEERT sector. On the night of the 15th inst previous movement orders being cancelled, all guns & personnel were withdrawn from the line & batteries moved into billets at PIGBROUCK 7.20.c.3.3. Later in the month & moving to ELVERDINGHE & acting under orders of R.A. II Corps, arrangements were made to bring 12 T.M's into action in the LANGEMARCK sector in support of 90th Belgian Divisions, were completed on the night of the 20th/21st and on the morning of the 28th a most successful shoot was carried out, each battery firing 200 rounds on selected targets with splendid results. Several casualties were sustained later in the day the enemy were forced to retire and T.M's were withdrawn from the line. Personnel were divided into parties and attached for duty to 36th D.A.C.	

Order of Battle. — 153rd Bde. & 143rd Bde. R.F.A.
D.T.M.O. 36th Div Lieut. (A/Captain) L.W. Fox. M.C. West Riding Regt. (T.C.)
X/36 17 Scottish Bty/Cmfd Lieut (A/Captain) J. CUTHBERT M.C. R.F.A. (T.C.)
Y/36 " " " " " Lieut (A/Captain) L.N. YINEN M.C. R.F.A. (T.C.)

WAR DIARY
or
INTELLIGENCE SUMMARY

Army Form C. 2118.

Place	Date	Hour	Summary of Events and Information	Remarks and references to Appendices
	Sept			
	1		Lieut R.M. Macnamara & 10 O.R's X/36. T.M.B. detached for duty at ammunition dump. ST JANS CAPPEL	
			3/Lieut J.J. Thompson & 20 O.R's attached to 173rd Bde T.M.B. for duty. Lieut A.G.S. Gosling & 20 O.R.s Y/36 attached to 153rd T.O. da. R.F.A. for duty. 1 O.R. Y/36 proceeded on leave. 1 O.R. "X" returned from Corps Rest Camp.	
	2		1 O.R. from each battery proceeded to II Army Rest Camp. Lieut E.P.M. Buchanan & 5 O.R's "Y" detached for duty at dump S.15 a 8.8.	
	3		1 O.R. Y/36 returned from leave.	
	5		1 O.R. from each battery proceeded on leave. H O.R.s "Y" detached for duty at ammunition dump at TRISCOTT HOUSE	
	6		6 O.R.s "X" " " " " with 36th D.A.C.	
	9		All personnel repair their respective batteries. Macnamara proceeded on leave.	
	10		Bde. batteries moved forward to S.12.c.4.6.	
	11		Capt. Vivier M.C. proceeded on leave to Paris.	
			1 O.R. "X" proceeded on leave to U.K. 1 O.R "X" returned from leave	
	12		1 Officer & 20 men from each battery commence work on positions in the line	

Army Form C. 2118.

WAR DIARY
or
INTELLIGENCE SUMMARY
(Erase heading not required.)

Instructions regarding War Diaries and Intelligence Summaries are contained in F. S. Regs. Part II. and the Staff Manual respectively. Title pages will be prepared in manuscript.

Place	Date	Hour	Summary of Events and Information	Remarks and references to Appendices
	13		1 OR "X" proceeded on leave to UK	
	15		All guns personnel withdrawn from the line — 1 OR "X" proceeded on leave	
			Ready from each battery proceeded in advance to billets at PIEBROUCK R20c 3-3	
	16		Remaining personnel to billets move to R20c 3.3.	
	17		1 OR "X" proceeded on leave. 1 OR "Y" returned from leave	
	18		1 OR "Y" " " " "	
	20		1 OR "X"	
	22		Both batteries move by motor lorries to ELVERDINGHE	
	23		Capt Vinson returned from Paris (leave). 1 OR "X" proceeded on leave to UK	
	26 25/26		2 OR "X" killed, 1 wounded. Lieut Newmann returned from leave	
			1 OR from each battery proceeded on leave to UK	
	27		2 OR "X" proceeded on leave. 2 OR "X" [return] from leave	
			1 OR "X" rtd from leave	
	28		Both batteries very active, most successful shoot, 3 casualties sustained	
			1 OR "Y" killed & 2 OR wounded. 1 OR "X" proceeded on leave	
			Capt J. Buttart M.C. proceeded on leave	

Army Form C. 2118.

WAR DIARY
or
INTELLIGENCE SUMMARY.
(Erase heading not required.)

Place	Date	Hour	Summary of Events and Information	Remarks and references to Appendices
	29		1. O. "X" proceeded on leave.	
	30		2. Officer + 20 O.R. "X" attached to 143rd Bde R.F.A. for duty.	
			2. " " " " " 152nd " " "	
			2. " " remaining personnel " 36th J.A.C. for duty	
			Casualties during month. — Killed Wounded	
			" " to Personnel " 3 3	
			" " Equipment — Nil	

[signature] Captain
for O.C. H.Q. 36th Division

Army Form C. 2118.

WAR DIARY 36 Div. T.M. Btys.
or
INTELLIGENCE SUMMARY.
(Erase heading not required.)

Vol. 28

36th Divisional Trench Mortar Batteries

October 1918

War Diary

Appx Sheet 28
29

Army Form C. 2118.

WAR DIARY
or
INTELLIGENCE SUMMARY.
(Erase heading not required.)

Instructions regarding War Diaries and Intelligence Summaries are contained in F. S. Regs., Part II. and the Staff Manual respectively. Title pages will be prepared in manuscript.

Place	Date	Hour	Summary of Events and Information	Remarks and references to Appendices
Pt Shut 28	1		Batteries still attached to 153rd & 193rd Brigades	
	5		1 O.R. "A" Battery killed in action whilst attached to 153rd Brigade	
	6		1 O.R. "A" & 1 O.R. "B" proceeded on leave to U.K.	
			1 O.R. "A" returned from leave	
			5 O.R. "A" & 1 O.R. "B" returned from leave to Battery	
			4 Reinforcements posted to "A" Battery	
	7		All personnel withdrawn from Brigades to BECELAERE	
	8		Commenced training at I.24 & 25.45	
			2 O.R. "A" & 2 O.R. "B" proceeded on leave to U.K.	
			1 O.R. "A" returned from leave	
	9		Lieut A.G.S. Ingleby proceeded on leave to U.K.	
			Fired 45 rounds on Gold Flake Farm h.19 c 02.90.	
	11		1 O.R. "B" proceeded on leave	
	13		Fired 110 rounds on GOLD FLAKE FARM & wire at h.19 t 05.30	
	14		Started to follow infantry with two mobile mountings	
			Fired 16 rounds from MOORSEELE ordering two machine guns	
			Camped the night at SILVER FARM h.22 t.	

WAR DIARY
or
INTELLIGENCE SUMMARY.

(Erase heading not required.)

Army Form C. 2118.

Place	Date	Hour	Summary of Events and Information	Remarks and references to Appendices
Bgf Sheet 29	14		Placed two mortars in action at G.19.d.95.15 with 30 rounds	
	15.		Fired 30 rounds in barrage for attack on GULLEGHEM. Camped at G.14.c.6.2.	
	16.		Fired 34 rounds from H.95.a.4.5. at H.3.a.8.9. to arrest infantry & engineers to cross the L.y.s. After 34 rounds fired H5 rounds on same targets to cover advance of own infantry. Camped at G.16.d.9.3.	
	17		Returned to 28/63.d.1.8.	
	18		Marched to B.13.t.4.4.	
			Marched the 14½ with 9 mobile mortars & camped at C.20.a.40.25	
	20	15.00		
	21	10.30	Opened fire at targets C.22.a.3. Fired 12 rounds from ZESSEGHEM STN G28a	
		14.00	Placed 2 guns in action at C.21.t.4.6. for defence & fire at C.23.a.2.2. on S.O.S. Camped at C.26.t.82.93.	
	22.		Wagon line shelled. 5 mules killed & 3 wounded. Captain L.O.YNEN. M.C. Grenaded on leave to U.K. Rendered unenable till fresh ones arrived. Camped at C.26.a.4.2.	
	23.		Kept in close touch with attacking infantry, not called on to fire. Camped at I.11.a.4.6.	

Army Form C. 2118.

WAR DIARY
or
INTELLIGENCE SUMMARY.
(Erase heading not required.)

Place	Date	Hour	Summary of Events and Information	Remarks and references to Appendices
	25		Camped at 118d.1.4	
	26		Returned to BEVEREN	
	27		Marched to KNOCK M21 6 OR "x" & 2 OR "y" returns from leave	
	28		General cleaning up & Kit inspection	
	30		20 mm trench mortar battery attached to 153rd & 143rd Brigade T.M.	
	31		Lieut. J.J. Thompson left for a month's tuition as Instructor in Second Army T.M. School	
			Casualties during month	Nil
			" Personnel	
			" Animals	Mules 5
			" Equipment	Nil
			Battle Order	
			D.T.M.O. 36th Division Lieut a/Captain L.W. FOX M.C. West Riding Regt. T.C.	
			O/C X/36th T.M. Bty. Lieut a/Captain J. CUTHBERT. M.C. R.F.A. T.C.	
			O/C Y/36th " " Lieut a/Captain L.M. VINEN. M.C. R.F.A. T.C.	
				J Cuthbert Captain RFA
				D.T.M.O. 36th DIVISION

Army Form C. 2118.

WAR DIARY
or
INTELLIGENCE SUMMARY.
(Erase heading not required.)

War Diary

36th Divisional Trench Mortars

November, 1918.

Ref Sheet 29.

WAR DIARY
or
INTELLIGENCE SUMMARY.
(Erase heading not required.)

Army Form C. 2118.

Place	Date	Hour	Summary of Events and Information	Remarks and references to Appendices

At LAUWE

At the opening of the month the batteries were from the right:- 153rd, 193rd Bdes. A general inspection was made and general preparation was taken for the move forward. On the 3rd the batteries moved forward to billets at (19/M.16.4.2).

5th All personnel were attached to Brigades forward of billets at 01440.0.0. Preparation was being made to support the attack on the 8th

On the night 6/7th. 12 guns were taken into position at AUTRYVE at 18:00.

The following day positions were prepared and were camouflaged & carried out at 14:45.

On the 9th at Y.14.d.4.9 & Y.15.d.4.9 On the 9th 9th & 120 rounds were fired in increase accuracy of practice 12th batteries were attached to billets at M.16.4.2

On the following day the 193 batteries were attached to TOURCOING.

On the 19th the batteries were incorporated into the Second Army E.355 dated 1/11/18 & attached to Brigades i.e. "X" Bty. to 193rd Bde. R.F.A.

"Y" Batty to 153rd Bde. R.F.A. After on the month the batteries were

WAR DIARY
or
INTELLIGENCE SUMMARY.
(Erase heading not required.)

Army Form C. 2118.

Place	Date	Hour	Summary of Events and Information	Remarks and references to Appendices
			The following subjects taught - Arithmetic English Lewis French	
			Order Battn.	
			Lieut a/Capt L.W. York M.C. Wesley Riding Regt. TC ITMO 26th D[ivisio]n unseen	
			Lieut " J. Guthort M.C. TC R+A 9/8 X Batty	
			Lieut " E.N. Lucas M.C. TC R+A 9/8 "/ Batty	

Army Form C. 2118.

WAR DIARY
or
INTELLIGENCE SUMMARY.
(Erase heading not required.)

Place	Date	Hour	Summary of Events and Information	Remarks and references to Appendices
	1		Batteries at rest at KAUWE	
	2		General inspection	
	3		Fired into Lille/ots at M16c4.2.	
	4			
	5		General withdrawal from Brigades & moved forward to Lillelots at O14c0.0.	
	6		2 vickers guns taken into line and dumped at AUTRYVE	
	7		Positions prepared as follows "X" Bty behind houses at V8d 35.50 and 1/Bty behind houses at V8d 6.6.	
	7 midnight		180 rounds complete taken to Positions (15 rounds per gun).	
	8	8.45 pm	All guns reported in and shoot from V14d 7.5 to V15d 4.9.7. ceased fire at 6.0 p.m. Only 120 rounds fired owing to an excessive number of misfires.	
	9		All guns were withdrawn from the line	
	10		Batteries returned to Lille/ots at M16c4.2.	
	12		Moved to Lillelots at TOURCOING	
	13		Lieut. A.P. McA. Buchanan returned from leave	
	16		Lt A.G.S. Gosling posted to 193 Bde R.F.A. 2/Lt H.L. Farcell posted to 153rd	

Col R.F.A.

Army Form C. 2118.

WAR DIARY
or
INTELLIGENCE SUMMARY.
(Erase heading not required.)

Instructions regarding War Diaries and Intelligence Summaries are contained in F. S. Regs., Part II. and the Staff Manual respectively. Title pages will be prepared in manuscript.

Place	Date	Hour	Summary of Events and Information	Remarks and references to Appendices
	19		Battery rearmament in compliance with Second Army G.O.'s dated 1/11/18 & attached to 6 Brigade 1" & "B" Bty & 193rd Bde R.F.A. & "B" Bty C 153rd Bde R.F.A.	
	21		Capt. L.M. Vicars MC returned from leave	
	22-28		Period spent in training. rifle drill, gun drill, harness work, Classes started in Aptitude English Courses French & football matches in the afternoon	

Committee Nel

Army Form C. 2118.

WA 30 & 31

WAR DIARY
or
INTELLIGENCE SUMMARY.
(Erase heading not required.)

Army Neuyen

36th Divisional Train

Our Diary

December 1918.
January 1919.

Army Form C. 2118.

WAR DIARY
or
INTELLIGENCE SUMMARY.
(Erase heading not required.)

Place	Date	Hour	Summary of Events and Information	Remarks and references to Appendices
			At the beginning of the month, special attention was paid to Educational Training in both batteries of the Bde. Throughout the month, the following subjects being taught, English, Arithmetic, Civics, French. These classes were continued throughout the month. Particular attention was also paid to Recreational Training, i.e. Football, Running, Boxing, in the former & latter rounds games, all the men shared in remarkably keen interest. Military Training was also carried out with a view to general smartness, the correct handling of Arms & deportment whilst on the march.	
			Casualties. Nil.	

A.N. Vuan
Captain RFA
for. OTMO. 26th Division

36th Divisional Artillery Trench Mortar Batteries

Army Form C. 2118.

WAR DIARY
or
INTELLIGENCE SUMMARY.
(Erase heading not required.)

January 1919.

Place	Date	Hour	Summary of Events and Information	Remarks and references to Appendices
TOURCOING	1-12.		Educational and Recreational Training continued.	
	1/3		Personnel of both batteries sent as Staff of Horse Collecting Camp COURTRAI. Stores left in charge of D.A.C.	
COURTRAI	13-31.		Working in COURTRAI. 30 N.C.O's & men demobilised during the month.	
			Casualties - Nil.	

J. Cuthbert Capt R.F.A.
O.C. X/36 T.M. Bty.

WAR DIARY
or
INTELLIGENCE SUMMARY

108th T.M. Battery.

Place	Date	Hour	Summary of Events and Information	Remarks and references to Appendices
MOUSCRON.	1919 Feb. 1st.		Unit still in MOUSCRON. Training and Educational work carried out. H.R.H.The Prince of Wales. visited and inspected the unit.	
	2nd.		Church Parades.	
	3rd.		Training and Educational Work carried out.	
	4th.		Unit bathed. Training as for the 3rd. inst.	
	5th.		As for the 3rd inst.	
	6th.		As for the 3rd inst.	
	7th.		As for the 3rd inst.	
	8th.		As for the 3rd inst. and Medical Inspection.	
	9th.		Church Parades.	
	10th.		Educational and Recreational work.	
	11th.		Unit bathed. Mortar cleaning and inspection.	
	12th.		As for the 10th inst.	
	13th.		As for the 10th inst.	
	14th.		As for the 10th inst.	
	15th.		As for the 10th inst.	
	16th.		Church Parades.	

Army Form C. 2118.

WAR DIARY
or
INTELLIGENCE SUMMARY.

(Erase heading not required.) 108th T.M. Battery. 36th (Ulster) Division.

Place	Date	Hour	Summary of Events and Information	Remarks and references to Appendices
MOUSCRON.	1919 Feb. 1st.		Unit still in MOUSCRON. Training and Educational work carried out. H.R.H. The Prince of Wales. visited and inspected the unit.	
	2nd.		Church Parades.	
	3rd.		Training and Educational work carried out.	
	4th.		Unit Bathed. Training as for the 3rd. inst.	
	5th.		As for the 3rd inst.	
	6th.		As for the 3rd inst.	
	7th.		As for the 3rd inst.	
	8th.		As for the 3rd inst. and Medical Inspection.	
	9th.		Church Parades.	
	10th.		Educational and Recreational work.	
	11th.		Unit Bathed. Mortar cleaning and inspection.	
	12th.		As for the 10th inst.	
	13th.		As for the 10th inst.	
	14th.		As for the 10th inst.	
	15th.		As for the 10th inst.	
	16th.		Church Parades.	

Army Form C. 2118.

WAR DIARY
or
INTELLIGENCE SUMMARY.

(Erase heading not required.)

Instructions regarding War Diaries and Intelligence Summaries are contained in F.S. Regs., Part II. and the Staff Manual respectively. Title pages 108th T.M. Battery. will be prepared in manuscript. 36th (Ulster) Division.

Place	Date 1919. Feb.	Hour	Summary of Events and Information	Remarks and references to Appendices
	17th.		Educational Work and Recreation.	
	18th.		Owing to Demobilization of Officers and Other Ranks, no further training carried out.	
	19th.		Inspections of Arms and Billets.	
	20th.		Unit Bathed. Mortar cleaning and inspection.	
	21st.		No work carried out owing to stage of Unit on 18th inst.	
	22nd.		As for the 21st inst.	
	23rd.		Church Parades.	
	24th.		As for the 21st inst.	
	25th.		As for the 21st inst.	
	26th.		As for the 21st inst.	
	27th.		Other Ranks returned to their respective Battalions for duty. Cadre (1 O.R.) and stores attached to 108th Infantry Brigade Head Quarters.	
	28th.		Officer Commanding Unit (Captain C.S. DOYLE.) Posted to and joined the 12th Royal Irish Rifles.	

(signature) Captain.
Officer. Commanding.
108th Trench Mortar Battery.

Army Form C. 2118.

WAR DIARY
or
INTELLIGENCE SUMMARY.

(Erase heading not required.)

Instructions regarding War Diaries and Intelligence Summaries are contained in F. S. Regs., Part II. and the Staff Manual respectively. Title pages will be prepared in manuscript.

108th T.M.Battery. 36th (Ulster) Division.

Place	Date 1919.	Hour	Summary of Events and Information	Remarks and references to Appendices
	Feb.			
	17th.		Educational work and Recreation.	
	18th.		Owing to Demobilisation of Officers and Other Ranks. No further training carried out.	
	19th.		Inspections of Arms and Billets.	
	20th.		Unit Bathed. Mortar cleaning and inspection.	
	21st.		No work carried out owing to state of Unit on 18th inst.	
	22nd.		As for the 21st inst.	
	23rd.		Church Parades.	
	24th.		As for the 21st inst.	
	25th.		As for the 21st inst.	
	26th.		As for the 21st inst.	
	27th.		Other Ranks returned to their respective Battalions for duty. Cadre (1 O.R.) and stores attached to 108th Infantry Brigade Head Quarters.	
	28th.		Officer Commanding Unit (Captain C.B.LOYLE.) Posted to and joined the 12th Royal Irish Rifles.	

[signature], Captain.
Officer, Commanding
108th Trench Mortar Battery.

www.ingramcontent.com/pod-product-compliance
Lightning Source LLC
Chambersburg PA
CBHW081538160426
43191CB00011B/1784